PREACHING
EVANGELISTICALLY

PREACHING
EVANGELISTICALLY

PROCLAIMING THE SAVING MESSAGE OF JESUS

AL FASOL, ROY FISH, STEVE GAINES, AND RALPH DOUGLAS WEST

BROADMAN
& HOLMAN
PUBLISHERS

NASHVILLE, TENNESSEE

Ten-Digit ISBN: 0–8054–4057–7
Thirteen-Digit ISBN: 978–0–8054–4057–7

Published by Broadman & Holman Publishers
Nashville, Tennessee

Dewey Decimal Classification: 251
Subject Heading: PREACHING \ EVANGELISTIC WORK

1 2 3 4 5 6 7 8 9 10   10 09 08 07 06

Contents

Preface

Within ten days of each other, Steve Gaines and Ralph Douglas West visited me in my office at Southwestern Baptist Theological Seminary in Fort Worth, Texas. Each expressed his concern at the lack of books on preaching an evangelistic sermon. Each suggested we coauthor a book on the subject. Steve and Ralph are two of the finest students whom I taught during my thirty-two years on the faculty at Southwestern. The idea of being a coauthor with either one of them was appealing. The idea of being a coauthor with both of them was irresistible. Even though Steve and Ralph did not know each other, they agreed not only to include the other in the project but also to invite Roy Fish to be a fourth coauthor. Thus, *Preaching Evangelistically* was born.

The purpose of our book is to provide information on preaching evangelistically with integrity, with biblical accuracy, with appeal to contemporary listeners, and absolutely for the glory of God. Steve Gaines wrote chapters 1 and 3; he also provided the title for this book. Chapter 1 discusses the changing culture to which our timeless evangelistic message is to be preached. In chapter 3, basic steps in preparing the evangelistic sermon are presented.

Ralph Douglas West wrote chapter 2 in which he calls for careful deliberation in selecting a biblical text for the evangelistic sermon. Chapter 4, which I wrote, offers ways in which to measure the relationship between the sermon and its biblical text. I also wrote chapter 6, in which the delivery of an evangelistic sermon is discussed on the premise that the purpose of any sermon delivery is to *maximize the message and minimize the messenger.*

Roy Fish shares his expertise on giving an evangelistic invitation in chapter 5. Chapter 7 contains three evangelistic sermons that use the information in the first six chapters of our book.

As pastors and professors, we offer this book with the prayer that it will enhance the efforts of preachers, of teachers, of all who bear witness for Jesus in leading others to accept Him as their Lord and Savior.

We owe a special debt of gratitude to Wendy Davis, administrative assistant to Steve Gaines, who typed the manuscript. Her pleasant professionalism made the job easier for all of us.

Al Fasol

Chapter 1

The Setting of the Evangelistic Sermon

Steve Gaines

One of my favorite things to do with my wife is to eat at a nice restaurant. Donna is an excellent cook, but she enjoys periodically having someone else prepare a meal and then wash the dishes afterward. Though we both enjoy eating out, my wife and I often differ about the selection of a restaurant. Personally, I am interested primarily in how the food tastes. I do not care whether the tablecloths, the curtains, and the carpet are color coordinated. As long as the steak is tender and the salad is fresh, it does not matter much to me if the tables and chairs are old and the walls need fresh paint. But beauty and aesthetics matter to my wife. She is concerned as much with the environment of the restaurant as she is with the food. For her, the atmosphere in which the meal is served and eaten is a critical ingredient for enjoyment and intimacy.

Likewise, the environment in which an evangelistic sermon is preached is crucial if the preacher desires to win the lost to Christ. Thus, in this opening chapter, we will begin our study on preaching evangelistically by focusing on the setting in which the evangelistic sermon is preached. Several characteristics that should mark effective evangelistic services will be discussed. Also, key elements of a worship service that are instrumental in assisting the preacher to win souls from the pulpit will be suggested.

Characteristics of an Effective Evangelistic Service

Know Your Listeners

Some preachers study the Bible. Others study people and culture. Effective preachers analyze both. Why? Because the effective evangelistic preacher will preach differently to a group of senior adults than he preaches to a group of high school seniors. Likewise, he will preach differently to a group of unchurched, white-collar, upper-class people in suburban Los Angeles than he preaches to a group of church-oriented, blue-collar, middle-class people living in a rural area in the southeastern United States. Although the message of the gospel never changes, how it is presented should connect with the cultural persuasions and unique personalities of the people addressed.

Fishermen who are successful do not keep only one type of bait in their tackle boxes. Nor do they insist on using one technique as they attempt to land a catch. Sometimes they fish on the bottom of the lake or ocean. At other times they troll, allowing the bait to drag along as the boat moves forward. On other occasions they work the bait around trees or underwater debris. They have lures and jigs of many shapes, sizes, and colors. Why? Because different kinds of fish are attracted to different kinds of bait. Thus, if a preacher wants to be an effective "fisher of men" from the pulpit, he must know what kind of fish he is trying to catch and the most appropriate ways to reach them.

The bottom line is this: *Preachers need to think and speak like missionaries!* To be successful, we must learn the culture, customs, and "language" of those we are trying to reach. For instance, you are in for a rude awakening if you try to reach most of today's teenagers by singing two-hundred-year-old hymns and preaching out of a four-hundred-year-old version of the Bible. That, my preacher friend, is definitely "poor fishing." Indeed, I love the great hymns of the church. I also have read the King James Version of the Bible through several times, and I personally appreciate it. These have their place. But they are not always the best way to reach certain groups. Get to know the people you are trying to reach for Christ. Sing Christ-honoring music to which they can relate. Use a version of the Bible they will understand. Remember, Jesus never spoke English!

It will be a great day when the preacher asks himself these questions: What are the people whom I am trying to reach?

What are their religious backgrounds? What kind of music do they prefer? What is their level of education? What are their predominant cultural customs? What do they like and dislike? When you start evaluating these and other issues like them, you will be well on your way to being more effective in making an initial evangelistic contact with your audience.

Focus on God, Not Man

The most important emphasis of a worship service is focusing on God. Worship services should be God-centered, not man-centered. Those who lead in worship will do well to steer clear of elaborate introductions of those who sing solos, lead in prayer, etc. Elaborate introductions of preachers should be avoided. The more we emphasize Jesus and deemphasize people, the more anointed a worship service will be. Worship services should not exalt people; they should exalt Jesus Christ. Likewise, worship services should not be designed primarily to attract people. Instead, they should seek to attract the manifest presence of God. When He "shows up," *He* will attract the people. "In [His] presence is fullness of joy" (Ps. 16:11 NNAS).

While evangelistic churches should try to be seeker friendly, their priority is to be Savior focused. We should strive to be gracious to those present in a worship service, providing comforts such as good lighting, relaxed seating, and appropriate temperature. But we should never focus on the people who are attending the worship service to the neglect of God. Jesus said that if we will worship and seek *Him* in spirit and truth, He will in turn seek *us* to be His worshippers (see John 4:23–24). If people leave a worship service saying, "What a preacher!" "What a sermon!" "What a choir!" or "What a church!" then we have failed. But if they leave a worship service saying, "Hallelujah, what a Savior!" then we have succeeded!

Present a Warm Atmosphere

Evangelistic preaching is most effective in a friendly, hospitable environment. Someone has said, "You cannot hatch eggs in a refrigerator." Likewise, you cannot expect to see people converted to Christ in a cold, inhospitable setting. Those who attend an evangelistic service should be met by greeters (in the parking lots and at every door) and ushers who welcome them warmly after they enter the place of worship. Christians in attendance should be sensitive to the presence of lost people in the service and seek to be cordial to everyone sitting near them.

Those who lead in worship should be genuinely enthusiastic and positive. The preacher should convey an inviting, positive, encouraging message through his facial expressions, the tone of his voice, and the content of his message. After all, the word *gospel* means "good news." The preacher should emphasize the salient demands of the gospel without shouting and snarling at his listeners. When the atmosphere is warm and friendly, people are more receptive to what the preacher has to say. "The wise in heart will be called understanding, and sweetness of speech increases persuasiveness" (Prov. 16:21 NNAS). Evangelistic preachers are called to "feed the sheep," not "beat the sheep."

Emphasize Jesus

If we want to win people to Christ through our preaching, we need to intentionally focus on Jesus Christ. We need to speak the name of Jesus frequently. The words *God*, *Lord*, and *Christ*, are all biblical, but there is something particularly powerful about the name of *Jesus*. That is why the angel said to Joseph (stepfather of Jesus), "You shall call His name Jesus, for He will save His people from their sins" (Matt. 1:21 NNAS). It is also the reason Peter said, "And there is salvation in no one else; for there is no other name under heaven that has been given among men by which we must be saved" (Acts 4:12 NNAS). The name *Jesus* literally means "God is salvation."

The worship music prior to the evangelistic sermon should highlight Jesus Christ. Songs that speak His glorious name are powerful and persuasive tools for softening the hardened hearts of lost sinners. Whether it is a familiar hymn that says, "My *Jesus* I Love Thee," or a less traditional song that says, "*Jesus, Jesus, Jesus*, there's just something about that name," or a more contemporary chorus that says, "My *Jesus*, My Savior, Lord there is none like You," music in an evangelistic setting should magnify the name above all names—the name of Jesus.

Likewise, throughout his sermon, the evangelistic preacher should focus on the death, burial, and resurrection of Jesus. He should talk about the cross and the redemption that Jesus purchased for lost sinners. C. H. Spurgeon, who preached to about six thousand people each Sunday morning for almost forty years in the 1800s in London, concurs by saying:

Let your sermons be full of Christ, from beginning to
end crammed full of the Gospel. As for myself, brethren, I cannot preach anything else but Christ and His
cross, for I know nothing else, and long ago, like the
apostle Paul, I determined not to know anything else
save Jesus Christ and Him crucified. . . . Preach Jesus
Christ, brethren, always and everywhere; and every
time you preach be sure to have much of Jesus Christ
in your sermon. . . . We preach Jesus Christ to those
who want Him, and we also preach Him to those who
do not want Him, and we keep on preaching Christ
until we make them feel that they do want Him, and
cannot do without Him.[1]

In the most precise sense, evangelism is the proclamation of the gospel. The word "evangel" is a trans_litera-
tion of the Greek word *euaggelion,* translated *gospel,*
which is a contraction of the Anglo-Saxon term *god-
spell,* meaning good tidings or good news. The New
Testament evangel referred to either the good news that
Jesus preached (the proclamation of the kingdom of
God) or to the good news about Jesus, who was both
the announcer and the revelation of the kingdom.[2]

Herschel H. Hobbs, longtime pastor of First Baptist Church,
Oklahoma City, also stressed that the message of evangelistic
preaching must center in the life and work of Christ.[3] We should
emphasize His virtuous life, His vicarious death, and His victorious resurrection. According to the apostle Paul, these are

the essential facts that constitute the gospel (see 1 Cor. 15:1–4). Like Philip, we must open our mouths and preach Jesus to a lost world (Acts 8:35). What greater news could one man tell other men?

Emphasize Participation, Not Performance

People today do not come to church to be entertained. The truth is that the world can entertain them better than the church can. Through television, videos, movies, and the Internet, people are exposed to the highest level of artistic performances and productions. When they come to church, they are looking for something that Hollywood cannot give them. That "something" is the presence and power of God. Evangelistic churches and preachers must remember that the world will always be able to outsing, outspeak, and outperform us. But the good news is that they will never be able to "out-God" us!

To promote a sense of audience participation, effective evangelistic worship services should emphasize songs that sing *to* God instead of *about* God. Sing songs that address God directly. Sing, "My Jesus, My Savior, Lord there is none like You," or "I love you, Lord, and I lift my voice to worship You, O my soul, rejoice," or "You are good, You are good, and Your love endures!" Songs sung about God help *educate* people. Songs sung directly to God are more effective in helping people *encounter* Him.

Effective evangelistic preaching should also take place in an atmosphere that makes use of images. Because of television, people are more visionary than auditory. That is why, if at all possible, hymnals should be replaced with overhead screens of some sort. Large screens at the front of the sanctuary are preferred by a generation that has grown up going to movies and watching television. The words to the songs of worship should be shown on these screens.

This allows for the worship music to "flow" from one song to the next without having to stop for introductions and announcements of hymnal page numbers. Senior adults will enjoy being able to see the words that are larger on the screens than those printed in a hymnal. Also, the volume of the singing will increase when people are looking up at screens as they sing instead of looking and singing down into a hymnal. Musical purists might argue that screens prevent people from being able to read the music. But few people read the music when they use hymnals.

While screens may seem as uncomfortable as Saul's armor for some who "have not tested them," preachers who want to reach people in today's society should force themselves to become comfortable with them. Screens help engage more of the worshippers' senses and aid in gaining and keeping the attention of those in the congregation. The "listeners" become "seers," which enhances participation and increases involvement and interest. The pastor's sermon title and main points should also be shown on the screens along with supporting Scriptures.

Screens also solve the problem of not being able to read Scripture publicly with the entire congregation because of the many different Bible versions among the people. With overhead screens the preacher can display any version of the Bible he prefers and ask the congregation to read along with him at any given point. This one element enhances participation.

Reverence? Yes! Formality? No!

Those who would reach people for Christ in the coming years must realize that our society is becoming less formal. Churches that would reach people for Christ also should avoid excessive formalities such as having their preachers, worship leaders, deacons, and choir members making a grand entrance by "filing in" at the beginning of a worship service. The preacher and other leaders should not bring attention to themselves through such pompous displays of ceremony. The preacher could well be one of the greeters mentioned earlier. Then, as the service begins, the preacher should be seated near the front. When the time comes for the preacher to speak, he can move from the pew *among the people* before proclaiming the message.

Worshippers today should be allowed to worship by clapping and lifting their hands to the Lord. When worshippers hear something they like in a sermon, they are much more likely to applaud than to say "Amen." They are also likely to shut their eyes and lift their hands to the Lord when singing a praise song. While no person should ever be coerced to clap or lift his hands to the Lord, there should always be complete freedom in our worship services for people to participate in these biblical methods of worship (see Neh. 8:5–6).

For older generations who were taught to "be still and quiet" in church, these suggestions might seem irreverent. But reverence and silence are not the same thing. A person lying in a casket is being still and quiet, but this is not because he is being reverent. Preachers who want to reach people must not allow themselves or their congregations to get hung up on such incidentals. Sing the great hymns of yesteryear, and sing the great choruses of today as well.

A Suggested Format for an Evangelistic Service

What kind of worship service is conducive for preaching an effective evangelistic sermon? I believe such a worship service should begin in corporate prayer. It is good to invite people to gather at the front of the worship center for a time of prayer led by the person who will be preaching the evangelistic message. The musicians should play softly while the people pray along with the preacher as he leads them. The musicians should select a song that the minister of music or the pastor can lead the congregation in singing immediately after the prayer is finished.

After prayer, a brief time of welcoming guests should follow. The preacher or someone else who is warm and enthusiastic should lead in the welcome time. It is best not to point out who the guests/visitors are at this point. Many churches do this, but I believe they are risking embarrassing their guests. Some ask their guests to sit while the members stand. Other churches even ask guests to wear lapel pins to indicate that they are indeed visitors. In my opinion, churches should not isolate their guests that way.

Instead, they should have a perforated piece of paper attached to the church bulletin which requests pertinent biographical information. Ask the guests to fill out these forms, tear them off the bulletin, and give them to an usher at the conclusion of the service. Tell them in exchange they will receive a complimentary packet that contains information about the church and a gift (perhaps a sermon tape/CD or a tape/CD of music by the choir and orchestra). Our church made these simple changes years ago, and the number of visitors who gave us the biographical data we requested more than tripled!

During the welcome time, the first song of the worship service should be played by the orchestra or the praise band. After the people have greeted one another, the minister of music should begin singing the song being played, asking the congregation to join in. This makes for a smooth transition from the prayer time, into the welcome time, and into the praise element of the service.

The service should then continue in an uninterrupted period of musical praise (between fifteen and twenty minutes). The songs that are sung should be a blend of the traditional hymns (teenagers and children need to learn them) and the newer choruses (adults of all ages need to learn them). Years ago I realized that God put a hymnal in the middle of the Bible. It is called the book of Psalms. But I noticed that He gave us only the words to these songs without also giving us the original musical accompaniments by which they were sung. In that way, every generation is able to "sing to the LORD a new song"

(Ps. 149:1 NNAS) by singing the same biblical text while using different musical scores that are culturally relevant to both the singers and listeners.

Billy Graham, one of the greatest evangelistic preachers of all time, has always used a blend of the old hymns and contemporary music. Though Dr. Graham is over eighty years old at the time of this writing, he is wise enough to utilize contemporary Christian groups to sing special music at his evangelistic crusades. In one of Dr. Graham's recent evangelistic crusades, a group known as Mercy Me sang their popular song, "I Can Only Imagine." At the conclusion of the song, the audience, young and old, applauded with enthusiasm. In that same worship setting, the congregation also sang the old hymns, "Amazing Grace" and "Just As I Am." If we want to reach our children and grandchildren for Christ, we must use the newer songs as well as the older hymns.

The music that best serves evangelistic preaching should be aimed at the heart as well as at the mind. As a rule it is best for the musical praise to begin with songs that have an upbeat tempo and then taper to a slower pace as the singing draws to a close. All of the lyrics of the songs should be biblically based and theologically sound.

The congregational praise should be followed by a special song offered by the choir (and orchestra if possible). Again, soloists should not be introduced publicly. Their names can appear in the bulletin if people want to know who they are. It is more effective if the special music and the theme of the sermon are related. It is frustrating to get up and preach on the death of Christ immediately after the choir has sung about His second coming! A little communication between musicians and the preacher will go a long way toward solving this problem.

After the music is over, the preacher should enter the pulpit and deliver a warmhearted, winsome, biblical message. Preferably, it should last between twenty and thirty-five minutes. Again, the preacher should engage as many of his listeners' senses as possible by using overhead screens to display his sermon title, text, and major points. He should use appropriate humor as well as relevant, engaging illustrations. He should maintain as much eye contact with his listeners as possible. If possible, he should at times leave the pulpit area and step to the level in the room where the people are seated, talking with them on their level physically as well as intellectually.

The evangelistic sermon should conclude with an open invitation to receive Christ as Savior and Lord. The listeners should be exhorted to make that decision public by coming forward to meet the pastor or a designated counselor at the front of the worship center. The preacher should share the gospel with the listeners, then lead them in a prayer a phrase at a time if they wish to receive Jesus as their Lord and Savior. After that time of prayer, the preacher should invite those who have accepted Christ and those who would still like to do so to come to the front and meet him for further counseling. The choir or the congregation should sing a hymn of commitment at this point to allow people time to walk to the front of the sanctuary to register their decisions for Christ.

Some preachers balk at such procedures. They say that "sinners' prayers" and public invitations are not biblical or necessary for people to be saved. I disagree. To preach the gospel of Christ without giving the listeners the opportunity to receive Christ as Savior and Lord on the spot is unthinkable! It is like telling a thirsty man about water but then denying him the opportunity to drink. To preach evangelistically is to preach persuasively for an immediate verdict. Our listeners should be asked either to receive or to reject Christ at the end of every message we preach.

The invitation is the most important time of the worship experience. No person should leave the sanctuary during the invitation unless there is a legitimate emergency. I also advise the preacher not to shut his Bible just before he extends the invitation. Closing one's Bible sends a nonverbal message that the important part of the sermon is over. We must preach all the way through our invitations.

Once the invitation is completed, financial offerings can be received and church announcements can be made. These should never come during the service itself because they tend to interrupt the flow of the Holy Spirit. Worship services should not be "choppy." There should be a natural progression from one phase to the next.

The pastor is the leader of the worship service. He and the minister of music should plan the order of service during the week and work out all details so there will be no surprises. Once the worship service begins, the pastor should be sensitive to the Holy Spirit's leadership. He may feel led to have a special time of prayer during the time of congregational singing or just before he preaches. He might even feel led to give an invitation for people to be saved before the sermon is preached. I have done this with great responses on several occasions.

Conclusion

An evangelistic sermon that is focused on Jesus Christ, culturally relevant, proclaimed in a worship service filled with heartfelt, biblical worship and praise, followed by a passionate, persuasive, polite, public evangelistic appeal is still a valid and vital means of winning lost people to Jesus. The setting of that evangelistic message is very important. Remember, the food is the most significant part of a meal. But how and where you serve it is crucial if you want to feed the masses with the eternal Bread of Life! And does that Bread still satisfy? Yes, indeed. Sinner, "Taste and see!" (Ps. 34:8 NNAS).

Chapter 2

Selecting the Text for an Evangelistic Sermon

Ralph Douglas West

Nothing is more important than evangelistic preaching. Around such sermons the kingdom of God grows, and the church finds joy in its preaching. It has been my chief concern over the last seventeen years at The Church Without Walls to select the most powerful biblical texts I can find to persuade men and women to come to life in the kingdom. The purpose of this chapter is to assist the working pastor and the witnessing Christian in the selection of biblical passages with the intent of seeing the kingdom born in the hearts of all those whom God wants to call His children.

The Need to Preach Evangelistically

Evangelistic texts abound throughout Scripture since the Bible is God's story of reconciliation. It is a book where the heart of a loving Father wants to call His wayward children back to the family. The Bible is a book driven by God's passion to reclaim a lost world. If God desires to redeem this world, our study and preaching must be on the message of salvation to a world that He desires to save. All who call themselves servants of the Word are mandated to preach the Word, and be God's witness. We who preach are called to mine the Scripture in hope of striking gospel gold and to show people that within the holy text there is the beauty of all that God wants to say to us about evangelism.

If evangelism is the good news about who God is and to whom we belong, it is incumbent on the communicator to be clear on what evangelism is. We must do this to keep from conveying a confused message to God's world. Evangelists sometimes become so zealous that they make some serious errors. There are some who preach a witness that assumes the purpose of evangelism is just to fill empty seats in a fledgling church. Jesus does instruct us in the parable of the banquet to go into the world. We are to "quickly, get out into the city streets and alleys. Collect all who look like they need a square meal, all the misfits and homeless and wretched you can lay your hands on, and bring them here." Our response to His instructions is, "Master, I did what you commanded—and there's still room." His response to our obedience is, "Then go to the country roads. Whoever you find, drag them in. I want my house full" (Luke 14:21–23 *The Message*).

If filling seats is considered the only purpose of sharing the gospel as good news, preaching can degenerate into a kind of institutional recruitment, with little or no reference to the eternal agenda of God. The messenger should never emphasize numbers over the importance of personal and individual understanding of who Jesus is. Nor should he play down Christ's redeeming presence in people's lives.

I often reflect on the postconversion experience of Paul the apostle as well as the intentional caring of people found in the documents of the early church, and how different the Christian world would be without them. If Ananias had disobeyed God's commissioning of him to minister to the new convert, we would not have the great doctrinal and pastoral letters to the church written by Paul. Although Paul was converted before Ananias came to see him, it was the faithfulness of this reluctant witness that made the difference in Paul's life. Now we are recipients of the great apostle's conversion and disciple-making ministry.

Everything therefore relates to the text that creates disciples from those who are self-willed and disinterested in God. When we choose an evangelistic text, we must be clear of our motives. To choose a text just to fill a building or a denominational report is wrong. Even if the text is good, our motives will not be.

In selecting the text for evangelistic sermons, we can fall into the trap of promoting some denominational cause above the importance of souls. This is often the case when a denomination institutes an evangelistic program for the purpose of increasing the statistics at the annual meeting. We often scuttle great evangelistic preaching in favor of pumping up our annual reports. Even when the statistics are good, the motives may be wrong. New believers are more than just the cold statistics that get recorded as baptisms, catechisms, and indoctrinations.

The purpose of evangelistic preaching and witnessing is to move persons—each too precious to wind up as a statistic—into the larger family known as the kingdom of God. Every Christian witness must understand the primary mission statement of Jesus: "The Son of Man came to find and restore the lost" (Luke 19:10 *The Message*). Souls are not to be won so we will look good in the annual reports. When we view each person as special, only then will we be able to preach evangelistically and authentically.

The text must stir the preacher if it is to stir the hearer. The preacher must believe the text if he is to become passionate in preaching it. No fervent sermon has ever hatched from the infertile eggs of casual concern.

George Hunter III supports this notion when he identifies the various types of ministries that are called evangelism. He categorizes their ministries under five headings: (1) Let us Help You, (2) Let God Help You, (3) Hear the Word, (4) Make a Decision, and (5) Become Christian Disciples.[1] Although these ministries are rooted in Scripture and help people, only one example— Become Christian Disciples—satisfies the New Testament model of evangelism, which is to communicate faith to people and make disciples who become followers of Jesus Christ.

Many congregations cater to the Make a Decision model of ministry, where the objective is to elicit from people a memorable point in time an act of the will called a decision. This is the salient objective of virtually all crusade evangelism—all the way from the mass crusades of Billy Graham to the one-to-one crusade evangelism of Campus Crusade. To their constituencies such evangelists report how many decisions were obtained at a specific time in a particular target audience. The text we choose should not be used to feed our baptism statistics; it should speak life to one soul at a time.

The model we should imitate is found in Christ's final words to His disciples. According to Matthew's Gospel, Christ's commission to His disciples is to "go out and train everyone you meet, far and near, in this way of life, marking them by baptism in the threefold name: Father, Son, and Holy Spirit. Then instruct them in the practice of all I have commanded you. I'll be with you as you do this, day after day after day, right up to the end of the age" (Matt. 28:19–20 *The Message*). The commission is to put people above numbers as a way of evangelism. Reach the person, and the numbers will count.

A simple reading about the apostolic witness in the book of Acts reveals the thesis that New Testament preaching was evangelistic. Their preaching bore witness to the resurrected Christ, who was the purpose of their preaching. Although the response to the gospel message in Acts was overwhelming, the people's acceptance of Christ was not Peter's aim.

The focus of his sermon on the day of Pentecost was to reveal to the hearers that Jesus was the Christ. Then when Peter walked meticulously through the witness of Old Testament Scripture, the people's hearts were trammeled like the hooves of horses breaking the ground beneath them. Their question was, "What shall we do?" This question was answered by the evangelistic reply, "Turn from your sins and turn to God, so you can be cleansed of your sins" (Acts 3:19 NLT). Sins are sinned one at a time. Sins, too, are forgiven one at a time.

Choosing an evangelistic text never forgets this fact. It is this singular forgiveness of sins that ushers in the time of refreshing into the life of those who believe. This is also the way people come into the kingdom. We do not have three thousand people being saved all at once; we have one person at a time being saved until the total reaches three thousand. The individual experiencing of God's forgiveness is the theme and theology of all evangelistic preaching.

The way Brooklyn Tabernacle Church of New York has received so much attention is an anomaly. Thousands of people flood into this church on weekends as well as for its midweek prayer meeting. The warm worship, winsome music, and multicultural mosaic make this church an attraction. But the most appealing distinction of this church is the stories of the people who make up the congregation. The church membership is a collage of drug addicts, alcoholics, sex-offenders, and society's rejects. The preacher should never forget the composition of the church when choosing a text. People who pile into this church feel accepted and are forgiven. Then they are used in ministry to reach persons like themselves. Regardless of their past failures, these persons have found a place of refreshing.

The Theology of Selecting a Text

Evangelistic preaching is needed because people do not know what to do with their sins. Many do not understand that they have sinned. An "I'm OK you're OK" attitude prevails. As a consequence most people are no longer troubled by their sins. If they consider sin at all, they regard it as a psychological hangover from their primitive past. Many believe they have outgrown all such notions. Words like *sin, guilt,* and *shame* are out of style in current culture. These antiquated terms have been replaced by a new terminology. Now we hear conversations peppered with a new psychological vernacular. Sin, once spelled S-I-N, is now spelled *phobias, neuroses, psychoses,* and *maladies.*

When choosing a text, see that text as more powerful than the secular ideas that stand against it. Andre Bustanoby, director of the Metropolitan Psychotherapy Group, tells of a letter he received from Jane, a sexually abused woman. Her pastor and Christian friends told her she would never heal from the wounds of sexual abuse until—in her words—"I forgive my father for what he did to me when I was a child."

"So I forgave him, or at least I thought I did, but when I sought reconciliation with him, he acted as though nothing had happened; he pretended we had a great relationship." By this point, Jane was so enraged at her father's denial that she walked out of the room.

She continued in the letter: "I finally had to stop seeing him. Not only did contact with him continually bring up the bad feelings about what he had done to me; I also felt a terrible strain whenever he acted like he had done nothing wrong."

More and more abused people as well as other victims of violent crimes are receiving the same sort of advice. This type of advice is not limited to the counselor's couch, but it can be heard from modern pulpits. Churches are increasingly becoming more psychological rather than theological. The text for an evangelistic sermon must be chosen to reply to a "know it all" psychology that has invaded the theology of secularized preaching.

People are often unable to forgive because they are confused by what forgiveness is. The two dimensions of forgiveness are theological and psychological. Theological forgiveness, according to Bustanoby, "makes possible the full reconciliation of the offended and the offender. Theological forgiveness requires that the offender see his need of forgiveness. 'If we confess our sins, [God] is faithful and just to forgive us our sins' (1 John 1:9 KJV). Psychological forgiveness, on the other hand, does not receive full reconciliation, although it releases the offended party from the pain of the offense. It allows individuals like Jane to carry on at least a civil relationship with others. In the end, though, it helps more with the health of the individual than the wholeness of the relationship."

It appears that many of our churches are moving away from the evangelical center. They fail to select texts that preserve this great evangelistic heart of the kingdom and are sliding dangerously to the margin toward an "I'm OK, it's OK, you're OK" posture. I am aware of this psychologizing when sermons are preoccupied with multiple self-help themes. The American pulpit is obsessed with being relevant. So we prepare our sermons not to hook the hearer with a relevant statement. Rather, we preach an entire message on "How to Be Happy" or "How to Find the Mate of Your Dreams." We often sound more like therapists than preachers.

The purpose of selecting the evangelistic text is to allow the text to address these felt needs and other issues without compromising the biblical intention. Felt needs are real needs to the person who has them. Our purpose as preachers is to bring those persons face-to-face with the God who can meet those needs.

The poet T. S. Eliot looked deeply into humanity's problem with sin in a conversation in his work entitled *The Cocktail Party*. Eliot pictured a woman named Celia talking to her psychiatrist, Reilly, about something she had done that was really bothering her conscience. Reilly asked her, "What was your family's point of view about the word *sin?*" She replied that she had been taught to disbelieve in it, to think of misbehavior as simply "bad form," and to regard anyone who was overly concerned with sin and guilt as "a bit kinky." Still the guilt remained long after she had jettisoned every notion that sin really existed.

Sin went easily! But she admitted that she had not been able to dispose of her sense of personal failure so easily. She said, "I continue to be bothered by a feeling of uncleanness, and feeling of emptiness, of failure toward someone or something outside myself. And I feel I must . . . *atone,* is that the word? Tell me, can you treat a patient for such a state of mind?"

Here is poignant evidence of our need to select the strongest text for evangelistic preaching because people do not know how to deal with what is ailing them internally or eternally. These same people have tried all types of formulas to get rid of the issue of sin that nags their quiet moments.

As a pastor I have observed several ways that people try to atone for their sins. The most prominent is the "God knows I'm human and that I'm going to sin" attitude. They continue, "At least God knows that I'm honest." This mind-set must be reprogrammed. The new messaging is, "Clear enough, isn't it, that we're sinners, every one of us, in the same sinking boat with everybody else?" (Rom. 3:19–20 *The Message*).

As we record over the misinformed data, the new outgoing message is: "But now that you've found you don't have to listen to sin tell you what to do, and have discovered the delight of listening to God telling you, what a surprise! A whole, healed, put-together life right now, with more and more of life on the way! Work hard for sin your whole life and your pension is death. But God's gift is real life, eternal life, delivered by Jesus, our Master" (Rom. 6:22–23 *The Message*).

These important evangelistic texts address humanity's need of a Christ who redeems. This is man's primary need—to get right with God. As a result, many felt needs are answered when our greatest need is addressed. Our greatest need is Christ in our life. Our basic need is God. As the Westminster Shorter Catechism reads, "Our chief aim is to worship God and to enjoy Him forever." What are we to do in the precious minutes of preaching to create an atmosphere for persons to experience God? Whatever we do, we ultimately credit our success or failure to the texts we choose for our sermons.

On the other hand, there are those who try to dodge personal guilt by putting the blame somewhere else. In the 1970s comedian Flip Wilson coined the phrase, "The devil made me do it." This phrase has become the mantra of many people. If people assume their sins are the result of someone else's behavior, they do not have to be responsible for what happens in their lives. The pews of many of our churches are filled with people with this type of fuzzy thinking.

Then there are those persons who attempt to deal with their sins by flagellating themselves. Ancient saints called this mortification; the idea was that if you suffered enough by your own hands, you could pay for your sins. This approach always tries to find just the right pain to fit the sin. We preach to many such misled people weekly. We encounter them daily in the marketplace. We cannot just hand them a "proof text answer." This would never fill the gaping cavity within their souls. A vision of the world's human landscape must be more than enough to drive us to preach the Word. We must be brought face-to-face with the need to return to preaching evangelistically. We must always seek to begin our preaching by choosing the best evangelistic text. The philosophies of the age are inadequate. They require a safe solution: evangelistic preaching.

Living in Search of the Evangelistic Text

As an interest in evangelistic preaching emerges, it addresses areas in a person's life that are desperate for attention. Because man is a spiritual being, material abundance will never satisfy his longings. What every person needs is to be told of his inability to live without God. We must prowl through the Scriptures until we encounter an evangelistic text that reveals man's need of God and says clearly that life is meaningless without Christ.

In a series of evangelistic messages, I sought to explain that God is the evangelist and we are to love people the way God loves us. This was the main objective, of the preaching series. To accomplish the preaching objective I limited the messages to three weeks. Then in prayer and Scripture reading I sought several passages that I felt would accomplish this objective.

The first message was entitled "Risky Business," taken from Romans 5:8. The sermon theme was this: Jesus enters our heart and rearranges the misplaced, displaced priorities of our lives. The second sermon was taken from John 4:39–42, "Have I Got a Story to Tell." The thesis of this sermon was this: We can change an unbelieving culture into a believing community by the power of our personal testimony. The final sermon was "Becoming a Chameleon Christian," taken from 1 Corinthians 9:19–23. The thesis was that to win some people to Christ we must adapt to the culture without adopting its lifestyle.

The intended progression of these messages was first to communicate to the hearer that it is God who saves; He is the evangelist. But for all the series I preach, I choose a text—an all-important passage—so God can do His work. Next was to lift Zacchaeus up as an example—Christ invites Himself into the private world of those whom He seeks, and on entry He rearranges the roles. He knocks as a guest but enters as a host, thus making necessary adjustments to our lives. Third, because of the new joy, we want to tell of God's goodness. No one can tell your story like you can. The challenge was for the hearers to leave the church, telling their personal stories of how Christ has changed their lives.

We live in a culture of disbelief. We cannot escape that reality. Neither should we want to run away from it. Therefore, as a church we can adopt certain relevancies to speak to the culture without adopting its lifestyle. All we say must be born in the preaching texts we choose. The role of the Christian is to witness about a Christ who can transform us into His image.

Above all else, these evangelistic texts must point people to the cross and reveal their need for spiritual recovery. This was important to Christ. In His farewell address Jesus left the earth looking into the face of His disciples and telling them to go into the world and preach the gospel and make disciples in all nations. This is a crucial truth for those who are interested in fulfilling His mandate to the church. Evangelistic preaching is God's only methodology for changing the world into His image.

What to Look for in Deciding on a Text

Step 1: Isolating the Kind of Texts We're Looking For

Many texts have been used—and many misused—in the effort to preach evangelistically. Remember this: just because a biblical text may mention salvation or the cross, its primary purpose may not be evangelistic in nature. For example, one text that is often used in reaching unchurched non-Christians is, "If I be lifted up from the earth, [I will] draw all men unto me" (John 12:32 KJV). This text clearly has to do with Jesus' death on the cross and the effects of his death on future believers. This may be a casual rendering rather than a primary text. I will explain the meaning of direct, secondary, and casual evangelistic texts a little later in this chapter.

Because of our familiarity with biblical texts and their usages among preachers, it is necessary for the preacher to identify the main objective of the text. When the main objective of the text is identified, it helps the preacher in at least two distinct ways. First, it helps him determine the way the author of the passage used the text within the context of his writing. Keep in mind that there is truth in the old cliché, "A text without a context is a pretext."

The second way the main objective of the text assists in the interpretation process is that it keeps the preacher focused on the main thing. Often in preaching one of two things can happen. A text may be misused to get the sermon in motion and then abandoned. At the point of this abandonment, the sermon may remain biblical, but it is no longer textual. A second fault is that the preacher sometimes forces the text to say something that the author of the text did not have in mind. Such isogesis puts the argument into homiletic method even as it removes it from the arena of textual authority.

Humpty Dumpty made a case for this type of interpretive violation when he declared, "When I use a word, it means just what I chose it to mean—neither more nor less."

"The question is," said Alice, "whether you can make words mean so many different things."

"The question is," said Humpty Dumpty, "which is to be master, that's all."[2]

Alice was correct in her asking. Words do have a wide variety of possible meanings, but the meaning they "exhibit in a particular context and also share in the public forum cannot be disregarded or arbitrarily used interchangeably." Alice is not alone in her inability to understand. Many who listen to sermons or read texts are left equally confused.

Alice was too puzzled to say anything, so after a minute Humpty Dumpty began again. "Impenetrability! That's what I say!"

"Would you tell me, please," said Alice, "what that means?"

"I meant by impenetrability that we've had enough of that subject, and it would be just as well if you'd mentioned what you mean to do next, as I suppose you don't mean to stop here all the rest of your life."

"That's a great deal to make one word mean," Alice said in a thoughtful tone.

"When I make one word do a lot of work like that," said Humpty Dumpty, "I always pay it extra."

"Oh!" said Alice. She was too puzzled to say anything here.

Alice's conversation with Humpty Dumpty sounds too much like confused parishioners who leave church questioning the integrity of the preacher's interpretation. Is that what the Scripture really means? This question and others surface from the lips of serious students of the Bible. The preacher is both communicator and interpreter. A primary role of the preacher is to interpret the Scripture according to the original author's intention. This exercise in locating intention may seem laborious at times.

Careful, deliberate study of the text is essential. This is where the preacher does his detective work. Each person reading this chapter has probably developed some sort of preliminary structure to choose the text. Briefly, here is how I get into the text. Once the text has been selected, I begin reading the text and parallel passages in the Hebrew or Greek. If you are not proficient in biblical languages, remember that many good, reliable modern English translations are available.

I also spend some time doing word studies. I want to avoid falling into Humpty Dumpty's philosophy of "paying words extra." Word studies can offer great insight, and the word image can create excellent illustrations. Additionally, I try never to bring my detective work to the pulpit. Rather, I want the fruit from my labor to be the aroma of the sermon. The word study also assists me in understanding the theological value of the Scripture passage. Many of the evangelistic sermons we hear don't have theological depth. I do not mean to imply that the evangelistic sermon should sound like a systematic theology lecture. I do mean that the theological understanding of God, man, and sin should be addressed.

Step 2: Sources of Evangelistic Texts

But what text are we to look for? What process is involved in selecting a text that will be certain in the evangelistic sermon?

Each preacher will vary in method. Some will follow the preaching lectionary. Some may even follow the "Hallmark" calendar (a nonbiblical index of the various Sundays like Mother's Day or the Fourth of July). While these special days are not without merit, the text may be summoned in a topical fashion that speaks to the people who celebrate these special days but do not know anything about the biblical text. Others will pay attention to the cycle of community events as the Holy Spirit reveals the sermon texts that might fit a particular community.

Whatever sermon mapping technique the preacher may follow, one thing is certain: Evangelistic preaching should be a part of the preaching planning for the growth, maturity, and development of the church and individual Christians.

I am often asked how I select the evangelistic text for a sermon. The obvious answer is from Scripture reading. The preaching minister should saturate himself in devotional reading of the Bible. Often devotional reading of Scripture reveals God as actively pursuing His children, which is the evangelistic thread of the Bible. If God is the Hound of Heaven, we should join in the hunt.

For a moment, allow me to step out of the traditional framework of evangelical preaching and suggest that there are other things that might serve as an evangelistic text. In preparing the evangelistic sermon, as theologian Karl Barth once commented, we should read the Bible with 20/20 vision. Read with one eye on the Bible and the other on the newspaper. Current events often serve as a reminder of our need of God's grace in the world.

Social problems are another interesting area to draw from. The constant craving of the young to be accepted draws them to gang or subcultural communities. This is a context that allows the preacher to state one's need to be in a family of acceptance. The unfortunate death of a community member could serve as a good context to preach an evangelistic sermon. A good context to draw on for the evangelistic sermon is national, state, and city elections. This is a good time to remind people that God alone is the ruler of the world.

I had waited for more than six months to return to my alma mater. President Ken Hemphill and the faculty and staff of Southwestern Seminary invited me to be the guest preacher for the fall revival in 2001. Finally the day arrived. On September 11, I boarded the American Airlines flight to Dallas-Fort Worth. While waiting for ground transportation to take me to the Southwestern campus, I grew anxious about the preaching invitation. Finally, I arrived on the campus on a beautiful Tuesday morning. My assigned host greeted me, and we whisked across campus to the Hogan House to prepare for morning chapel.

While I was knotting my tie, I was startled by rapid knocking at the door. *Surely, it's not time to go to chapel,* I said to myself. Annoyed, I answered the door, only to be met by a set of wide eyes. "A plane just crashed into the New York Trade Tower," he said. "Apparently, a neophyte pilot lost his bearings."

We were sorry to hear this and prepared to go across the campus to the president's office. Then suddenly, a second plane hit the tower. A burst of flames, smoke, and people jumping out of windows, others running frantically down the streets—all these were captured on camera right before our eyes. A cutaway to Washington, D.C., and another plane plummeting into the Pentagon weakened me. Then a plane down in the fields of Pennsylvania was more than we could take in. This was obviously no accident. Something sinister was happening before our eyes.

Moreover, this was the context for our long-anticipated fall revival. The surreal sight of 9/11 gripped everyone present. The solace of the morning dampened the flames of revival. Or did the events of the day poker the embers and ignite the fire of revival? Initially it did not seem this way. Then I could hear the words of William Cowper in my ear: "Judge not the Lord by feeble sense, \ But trust Him for His Grace \ Behind a frowning Providence \ He hides a smiling face."

As the chapel filled with students and faculty, I felt the burden of being God's witness. I recall the awesome obligation placed on me to bring God's message. I wept as I turned to the text. It was the mortar that brought hope. It always does. I stood and read from 1 Kings 17 and narrated the story of the prophet Elijah being alone at the Kerith brook. I reminded the theological community that while living beside a dried-out brook, the prophet depended on a scavenger to feed him. Elijah learned that day to depend on God in a place of uncertainty. The cutting place is where we are dependent on God's providence.

Although the text was not evangelistic in nature, it served an evangelistic purpose. It reminded us that in the unexpected difficulties of life, God can be trusted. Sometimes the evangelistic sermon will encourage the saved to be a witness to others about the surety of God's salvation. This is the *sine qua non* of evangelistic preaching to remind humanity, "This is how much God loved the world: He gave his Son, his one and only Son. And this is why: so that no one need be destroyed; by believing in him, anyone can have a whole and lasting life" (John 3:16 *The Message*).

What Do You Look for in Preaching the Evangelistic Sermon?

It has been my practice as a pastor to include a series of evangelistic sermons, based on authentic evangelistic texts, within the preaching schedule of my church. My motivation comes from the ministry of Jesus Himself. He declared that He had come to seek and to save those who are lost. Since reaching people who were without a relationship to God the Father was His objective, I believe this should be my preaching objective also.

Once I have decided to preach a sermon or a series of messages on evangelism, the first thing I do is to locate different Scripture passages that will best speak to the needs of those unreached people whose lives intersect my congregation. Then I begin to study those passages to be certain that I do not violate the biblical writer's intention for including these passages in the biblical text.

Every biblical writer wrote with a specific intention in mind. Understanding the author's purpose frees the preacher from guesswork so he can begin to shape the sermon according to the idea of the biblical writer. To ignore this simple principle is to ignore the text and therefore take liberties that were never

intended by the author. This notion weakens the text by allowing the preacher to place his entire emphasis within the "new
hermeneutic." There are many preachers who hold to this discipline, and it is recognizable in too much preaching today.

Here is a list of some of my favorite evangelistic texts. The
first is the story of the sinner friends who barnacled themselves
to Jesus. The biblical nickname of Jesus—"friend of sinners"—
is an important text. Luke 15 is a portrait of the extravagant
love of God. He is like a woman who loses her dowry and turns
the tables searching for her precious coin. He is like a shepherd
who searches for a sheep that strays from the fold. He is also like
a loving father who waits for grace to push his son back home.
What makes this chapter unique is that the theme of Luke is the
universal appeal of Christ.

Luke 15 also points out the reaction of many believers who
have not wasted their lives. And this chapter shows how conten-
tious we may become when a party is given in honor of a squan-
dering son. This one chapter reveals the love of God toward
His creation. We are reminded of the great love God has for us.
It also shows the way we are to rejoice for those who discover
God's amazing grace.

Here are just a few of my other favorite texts: Hosea 14;
Joel 2:12–14; Luke 14:15–24; Romans 5:6–8. Within each
passage there is the picture of a loving God and a needy person. Nothing can answer man's deepest longing but God.

The new hermeneutic allows the preacher to interpret a
biblical text with no concern about what the biblical writer
intended. This kind of preaching succeeds in one aspect. What

the original author intended can be given a different meaning altogether because he was far removed from the contemporary situation. The advantage of this method is that it allows the preacher liberties to speak to today's audience with more relevance. But the danger of this method is that it eliminates much biblical authority by ignoring the intent of that portion of Scripture in the first place.

Therefore, the first question to ask in locating a biblical text is this: Can you say that this passage of Scripture speaks directly to the subject of evangelism? To help you achieve this goal, a good working definition of what evangelistic preaching is may help. Also, what do you mean when you use the term *evangelism?* What does the Bible say about the subject in question? Remember one good way to interpret the subject is to let the Scripture interpret Scripture.

For instance, here are some biblical texts categorized by biblical authority. First are a few direct texts: Matthew 10:38–39; 13:1–23; Mark 1:40–45; Luke 15:11–32; John 3:1–17; 14:6; Acts 2:14–39; 8:26–37; Romans 1:14–17; 5:1–11; 10:9–10; Ephesians 2:1–10; 1 John 5:1–13; Hebrews 9:23–28. In each of these passages there is a direct correlation to the author's intended purpose for preaching evangelistically. These are a few recommended texts that can be preached with authority to reach people with the gospel of Jesus Christ. The benefit of these passages is that they speak directly to people's need of God's salvation.

Next is a list of secondary texts: Titus 3:1; 2 Corinthians 5:12–19; 2 Timothy 3:1–5; 2 Peter 3:3–7. This short list of texts should not be minimized because it is a gathering of secondary texts. A secondary text is one that supports the primary text to be given to the church with an emphasis on evangelism. The benefit of such passages is that they address a primary ecclesiological issue and simultaneously touch on the needs and benefits of salvation. Let the preacher sharpen his skills in selection so he may learn of the many texts that are dominant as well as those that have a subordinate purpose.

Casual References Misapplied

Finally, these are a few casual texts: Revelation 3:20; James 2:18–26; Galatians 5:1. A careful look at Revelation 3 gives us a picture of the church at Laodicea. The text is not a primary evangelistic text. The spiritual condition of the Laodicean church according to John was that the church was lukewarm—neither hot nor cold. Any serious coffee drinker knows that coffee is to be consumed only one way—hot. But this church in Asia Minor was neither hot nor cold. The only thing it was good for was to be spit out.

The passage concludes in verse 20: Christ stands at the door knocking. Any person who opens the door to Him, He "will come in . . . and dine with him and he with Me" (NKJV). The text speaks of Christ's power to convert the church back to her created purpose. Likewise, the power of Christ can convert the heart of man toward Him.

But the passage is not a good evangelistic text. The dominant purpose of the Revelation 3 passage is to address the spiritual condition of the church and her need to return to Christ. A subordinate purpose of the text is that it speaks to man and his need to come back to God, but it is not a text that should be used to talk about our obligation to witness.

Conclusion

At the end of the evangelism series previously mentioned, the calendar gifted me with an extra Sunday, so I decided to add a final installment into the sermonic series. The selected passage was John 20:31: "But these are written that you may believe that Jesus is the Christ, the Son of God, and that believing you may have life in His name" (NKJV). The tag on the text was, "You Have Made a Believer Out of Me."

The purpose of the message was to draw the hearers into the story of disbelieving Thomas. My thesis was that the real meaning of life is granted to those who believe Jesus is the Christ. I tried to describe Thomas carefully as a person who lived in a believing community and still did not believe, reporting to the congregation all the opportunities available to hear the good news about God yet not believe.

I held the suspension of Thomas's confession until the very end of the sermon. As the people listened with expectation, you could almost sense them pleading for Thomas to believe. What's going to happen to poor Thomas? Will he ever believe? Before Thomas declared, "My Lord and My God!" I tightened the tension once again by leaving Thomas disbelieving. Then I carefully crafted a one-sentence commentary on each chapter of the Gospel of John. When I got to chapter 20, I switched to

Thomas, looking desperate and delighted and confessing, "My Lord and my God!" (v. 28 KJV). Then thunderously, I ended the message with the words, "You have made a believer out of me!" The congregation leaped in excitement.

Next, I stood before the enthralled congregation and extended an invitation to those who now believed that Jesus is the Christ. The invitation is not an appendix to the sermon; it is a part of the sermonic process. As much attention should be given to the wording of the invitation as to the sermon itself. More than one hundred people walked forward and made a public confession, saying, "I believe!"

Selecting the evangelistic text can be like looking for a piece of border in a ten-thousand-piece puzzle. But when you select the right piece of the puzzle, it all begins to make sense. It also brings meaning and joy to those who have no purpose.

Chapter 3

Preparing the Evangelistic Sermon

Steve Gaines

Jesus was a preacher. When He began His earthly ministry, the Bible says, "Jesus came . . . preaching" (Mark 1:14). Jesus Himself said, "I must preach the kingdom of God . . . for I was sent for this purpose" (Luke 4:43). Although Jesus did indeed minister to the social needs of mankind in His day, His primary purpose for coming to earth was not to heal the sick, feed the multitudes, or clothe the naked. Rather, Jesus' priority was preaching the good news of the kingdom of God. He knew man's most important needs were—and still are—spiritual, not physical.

Jesus was also an evangelist. After He brought salvation to Zacchaeus in Jericho, Jesus said, "The Son of Man has come to seek and to save that which was lost" (Luke 19:10). Not only had He come to preach; He had come to preach evangelistically. Jesus, strictly speaking, was God's first evangelistic preacher. Many have followed His example, but no one has come close to surpassing His effectiveness. He was both the message and the messenger. He was the Word of God (John 1:1–2) who preached God's Word!

Every preacher should follow Jesus' example by preaching evangelistically. He should open his Bible and preach for the conversion of men, women, boys, and girls. He should expect people either to accept or to reject the gospel each time he shares it. The sword of the Spirit is the Word of God (Eph. 6:17). It is indeed a two-edged sword (Heb. 4:12). It has been said that, "God's word is 'two-edged' in that one side of the sword comforts the afflicted, while the other side afflicts the comfortable!" Indeed, the sword of God's Word divides all humanity (Matt. 10:34–36), forcing listeners into either belief or disbelief about the claims of Christ. The preacher literally stands between the sinner and eternity, offering him the gift of abundant, everlasting life in Christ. Thus, preaching evangelistically is both a daunting challenge and an awesome responsibility.

I once read of an effective rural preacher who was explaining how he prepared and delivered his sermons. He said, "First I pray myself hot, then I read myself full, then I turn myself loose!" He was right on target. Evangelistic preaching should come from both a hot heart and a full head. If the preacher prays without studying, his sermons will lack content. If he studies without praying, his sermon will lack power. The former is like shooting a blank without a bullet. The latter is like trying to shoot a bullet without gunpowder. The result is the same—the target is missed! Evangelistic preaching must include both passionate delivery and biblical content.

This chapter will focus on the first two of the country preacher's emphases: "Praying Oneself Hot," and "Reading Oneself Full." Another chapter in this book will deal with delivering the evangelistic sermon.

Pray Yourself Hot

Preparing evangelistic sermons should begin with prayer. Preaching should be the priority of the pastor's ministry, but prayer should be the priority of his entire life! Like Jesus, every preacher should rise early each day and spend time in communion with the Father (see Mark 1:35). He must also be ready and willing to pull aside from his busy daily routine to spend additional time in prayer (Luke 5:16). A preacher who rarely talks *with* God has no business trying to talk *for* God.

Pray for a Clean Heart

The preacher should begin preparing his sermon by preparing himself. Men look for better methods. God looks for better men. Unless the preacher is walking in purity with the Lord, his preaching is a sham and will prove to be powerless. The preacher must pray and ask the Lord to reveal any sin he might be stubbornly or secretly harboring in his heart. A good place to start is by praying Psalm 139:23–24, "Search me, O God, and know my heart; try me and know my anxious thoughts;

and see if there be any hurtful way in me, and lead me in the everlasting way" (Ps. 139:23–24). David's prayer in Psalm 51 is another text that can be prayed by every preacher who desires to be cleansed by God.

> Create in me a clean heart, O God,
> And renew a steadfast spirit within me.
> Do not cast me away from Your presence
> And do not take Your Holy Spirit from me.
> Restore to me the joy of Your salvation
> And sustain me with a willing spirit.
> Then I will teach transgressors Your ways,
> And sinners will be converted to You.
> (Ps. 51:10–13 NNAS)

David knew he would not see sinners converted until *after* he was cleansed and purified! When such prayers are prayed sincerely, the Holy Spirit reveals the preacher's sins so he can confess and forsake them and receive forgiveness (Prov. 28:13; 1 John 1:9). He should then ask the Lord to fill him afresh with the Holy Spirit (Luke 11:13; Eph. 5:18).

Preachers who harbor sin in their lives undermine their prayers. The psalmist said, "If I regard wickedness in my heart, the Lord will not hear" (Ps. 66:18). Rebellious preachers should not expect God to save lost people who listen to them preach. The servant of God must seek to maintain "clean hands and a pure heart" (Ps. 24:3–5) before God in order to be effective in the pulpit.

Pray for a Sermon Idea

After the pastor's heart has been cleansed by God, he should pray and ask the Lord to guide him concerning what he should preach. God said through the prophet Jeremiah, "But if they had stood in My council, then they would have announced My words to My people, and would have turned them back from their evil way and from the evil of their deeds" (Jer. 23:22). The Holy Spirit will guide the preacher regarding the selection of an appropriate text. In fact, as the preacher prays and reads the Bible, the text will seemingly "jump from the page," burn in his heart, and demand to be preached! More will be said about this later in this chapter.

Pray for Insight in Interpretation

Once his heart is clean and his text and sermon idea are secured, the preacher should pray for the Lord to enlighten him about the meaning of the biblical text. This should be done *before* the preacher studies the writings of others. Commentaries should indeed be consulted but not until after he has first written down his impressions, insights, and ideas from the text. This important step will keep his messages fresh and will prevent his sermons from being a boring collage of quotations from various commentators. God does not want His preachers to be mere parrots who mimic other men's thoughts and words.

As the Puritan preachers studied for their sermons, they would often pray, "More light, O Lord, more light!" Prayer brings the power of God's Spirit into the analysis of the text. God's Spirit inspired the text (2 Tim. 3:16), and He also promises to "guide [us] into all the truth" (John 16:13) as we study it.

In addition to praying for the Lord to guide him in biblical interpretation, the preacher should also pray that the Lord will assist him in crafting appropriate illustrations, determining sermonic application, and preparing an appropriate evangelistic invitation for the purpose of persuading his listeners to receive Christ as their Savior.

Prayer for Spiritual Conviction

Unless the Holy Spirit convicts lost people of their sins, they will not repent and be saved. The preacher's wisdom and oratorical skills are insufficient for the salvation of even one soul! Paul emphasized this when he said to the Corinthian Christians:

> And when I came to you, brethren, I did not come with superiority of speech or of wisdom, proclaiming to you the testimony of God. For I determined to know nothing among you except Jesus Christ, and Him crucified. I was with you in weakness and in fear and in much trembling, and my message and my preaching were not in persuasive words of wisdom, but in demonstration of the Spirit and of power, that your faith should not rest on the wisdom of men, but on the power of God. (1 Cor. 2:1–5)

God does not save people by means of human wisdom but through the preaching of the gospel centered in the cross of

Christ (1 Cor. 1:21). As preachers and other Christians pray for the lost listeners in their audiences, the Holy Spirit will convict many of those people of their sins, their lack of righteousness, and the fact that they will one day stand before God in judgment and give an account for their lives (John 16:8).

Prayerless preaching is a curse on any congregation. It is also the ultimate form of pride and presumption. When the preacher neglects the discipline of prayer, he assumes that he is capable of preparing and delivering a sermon without God's help. What folly! God uses our prayers to till and open the soil of the hearts of our listeners so that many of them will be receptive to the gospel seed when it is sown and planted through our preaching. When we preach without praying, the seed of God's Word is sown on hard soil and bears little or no fruit.

Read Yourself Full

While it would be impossible to overemphasize the importance of prayer for the preacher, it must also be pointed out that prayer alone is not enough to make for good evangelistic preaching. Unfortunately, much so-called evangelistic preaching has just been praying oneself hot and turning oneself loose without also having read oneself full. A preacher must not only pray but also study God's Word. He should "be diligent to present [himself] approved to God as a workman who does not need to be ashamed, accurately handling the word of truth" (2 Tim. 2:15).

Securing a Sermon Idea

Earlier we mentioned that as the preacher immerses himself prayerfully in the biblical text and diligently and systematically reads, studies, and meditates on the Scriptures, the Holy Spirit will cause him to be drawn to a specific text out of which a particular idea about that text will begin to surface in his mind and captivate his heart. A preacher should get his sermon ideas from the Bible! He should not procure a sermon idea and then try to find a text that fits his idea.

Nor should a preacher preach the sermons of other preachers. While it is acceptable to study the works of others, and even quote the works of others (acknowledging the sources and giving credit to whom it is due), it is never right to copy someone else's sermon and preach it as though it were your own. Such sermons enter through your eyes and exit your mouth without also passing through your head or your heart! God says, "Behold, I am against the prophets . . . who steal My words from each other" (Jer. 23:30). God does not need pirates in His pulpits who pilfer their messages from others. God wants His preachers to "[stand] in [His] council" and "then . . . [announce His] words to [His] people" (Jer. 23:22), mining their sermons from the bottomless quarry of God's Word, the Bible. We are to "work hard at preaching and teaching" (1 Tim. 5:17). God will not bless stolen sermons. They produce pygmy preachers and cheated congregations.

Not every biblical text lends itself to evangelistic preaching. But a conscientious preacher will not have trouble finding appropriate biblical texts that can serve as the basis for a great sermon that will be used to win souls. The following suggestions for appropriate texts and themes for evangelistic preaching come from Perry and Strubhar's excellent book *Evangelistic Preaching*,[1] intermingled with suggestions from this author as well.

- Old Testament texts dealing with the great themes of God, man, sin, suffering, judgment, and death.
- Old Testament prophetic texts, particularly those given by God immediately prior to His judgment upon Israel and Judah by means of exiling them to foreign lands.
- New Testament conversion experiences in the lives of such people as Zacchaeus (Luke 19), the Samaritan woman (John 4), the thief on the cross (Luke 23), the Ethiopian eunuch (Acts 8), Saul/Paul (Acts 9), Cornelius (Acts 10), and the jailer at Philippi (Acts 16).
- Events from the life of Jesus such as His birth, sinless life, atoning death, bodily resurrection, and imminent return.
- Great doctrinal themes from the Bible such as God, Christ, sin, salvation, election, heaven, hell, and the end of time, etc.
- Great Bible verses such as:
  Numbers 32:23—"Your sin will find you out."
  2 Kings 20:1—"Set your house in order, for you shall die and not live."
  Isaiah 1:18—"'Come now, and let us reason together,' says the LORD."
  Daniel 5:27—"'TEKEL'—you have been weighed on the scales and found deficient."

Matthew 7:13—"Enter by the narrow gate."

Matthew 27:22—"What shall I do with Jesus?"

John 3:7—"You must be born again."

John 3:16—"For God so loved the world."

Acts 3:19—"Therefore repent and return, so that your sins may be wiped away" (NNAS).

Acts 16:30—"What must I do to be saved?"

Romans 5:1—"Having been justified by faith, we have peace with God."

Romans 6:23—"The wages of sin is death, but the free gift of God is eternal life."

Romans 10:13—"Whoever calls on the name of the LORD shall be saved" (NKJV).

2 Corinthians 5:17—"If anyone is in Christ, he is a new creature" (NNAS).

- The "I Am" statements describing Jesus in John's Gospel:

    The Bread of Life (6:35).

    The Light of the World (8:12).

    I AM (8:58).

    The Door (10:9).

    The Good Shepherd (10:11, 14).

    The resurrection and the life (11:25).

    The way, and the truth, and the life (14:6).

    The true vine (15:1).

- Texts dealing with eschatological subjects such as the rapture of the church (1 Cor. 15:50–58; 1 Thess. 4:13–18), the Great Tribulation (Matt. 24:21; Rev. 6–19), the return of Christ (Rev. 19:11–16), the millennial reign of Christ (Rev. 20:1–6), the final judgment (Rev. 20:7–15), and the New Jerusalem (Rev. 21–22).

- Great invitations from the Bible such as:

    Exodus 32:26—"Who is on the LORD's side? let him come unto me" (KJV).

    Joshua 24:15—"Choose for yourselves today whom you will serve."

    1 Kings 18:21—"How long will you hesitate between two opinions? If the LORD is God, follow Him"

    Mark 1:15—"Repent and believe in the gospel."

    Matthew 4:19—"Follow Me, and I will make you fishers of men."

    Matthew 11:28—"Come to Me, all who are weary and heavy-laden."

    Acts 2:38—"Repent, and let each of you be baptized."

    Acts 2:40—"Be saved from this perverse generation!"

    Revelation 22:17—"Come . . . whosoever will" (KJV).

Developing the Functional Elements

Every evangelistic sermon should be organized. God is not the author of confusion. The extent of structure can vary from a strict outline to a thematic approach. However it is developed, the evangelistic sermon should be well planned and thought out with appropriate creativity and logic. It should, as a rule, include some sort of introduction, explanation, illustration, application, conclusion, and invitation.

Introduction. The significance of the introduction to an evangelistic sermon cannot be overemphasized. A sermon that begins poorly will probably end poorly. The first part of the sermon is very important. It sets the stage for all that follows. The evangelistic preacher should keep his introduction brief and not overwhelm his listeners with excessive information. It should also be interesting, arresting the attention of those who hear it. In fact, one of the best ways to make a sermon seem "shorter" to our listeners is to make it more interesting! Charles Spurgeon once said, "Dull preachers make good martyrs. They are so dry they burn well."[2]

An effective format for an introduction is (1) state the thesis sentence (central idea of the sermon); (2) share an illustration; (3) introduce the text (give the context as well as the burden of your message); (4) read the text; (5) announce the title and perhaps the main points (if applicable); and then (6) enter the body of the sermon. Once the introduction is given, the preacher should explain, illustrate, and apply the biblical text.

Explanation. Explanation deals with what the text meant in its original context and setting. The preacher must engage in an in-depth "historical, grammatical, and literary study of a passage in its context."[3] Explanation deals with the "then" part of the sermon and utilizes verbs in the past tense. For example, a sermon on John 3:7 could be explained by saying, "Jesus *was telling* Nicodemus that he *needed* to be born again." Note that the verbs are all past tense.

In all preaching, and especially in evangelistic preaching, the preacher should avoid biblical explanation that goes over the heads of his listeners. The average listener does not really care about the proceedings of the Nicene Council, nor is he interested in the fact that a certain word is actually a present passive participle. Save the theological jargon and Greek lessons for an academic setting, and explain the biblical text in language that common people can understand.

Illustration. Illustrations are very important in evangelistic preaching. Share an appropriate illustration. Paint a memorable picture with carefully crafted words. Share someone's conversion experience.[4] Illustrations are like windows. They should allow additional light to shine on the meaning of the text. The preacher must always be careful to use integrity in his illustrative material and avoid embellishing the facts. He should also avoid telling sad stories that do not relate to the text for the purpose of playing on the emotions of his listeners. It is the Holy Spirit that empowers preaching, not emotional exaggeration for the purpose of audience manipulation.

The best illustrations do not come from dated books of illustrations. It is better to give an illustration from personal experience, a biblical incident, or from common occurrences in everyday life to which the majority of people can readily relate. John Bisagno, who served as pastor of First Baptist Church, Houston, Texas, for thirty years, affirms this by saying,

> 95 percent of the preachers I listen to are telling me
> stories from Scotland or England and France about
> Lord Chancellory, vicar of England, or Baron "Von
> Whosoever" of Scotland in the seventeenth century.
> Get rid of those old sermon illustration books and get

into life. Read today's authors. Read modern books of
sermon illustrations. Read *People, Time, Newsweek, USA
Today,* and your local newspaper. Listen to the radio.
Listen to television, particularly the evening news. Get
among your people. Get out into the real world and find
real, live, relevant illustrations.[5]

While our listeners will seldom be able to recite our outlines
(even if our points all begin with the same letter!), they will
likely remember our stories and illustrations.

Application. Once the biblical text has been explained and
illustrated, it needs to be applied. Some preachers do not think
application is the preacher's responsibility. They say the preacher
should just explain the text and allow the Holy Spirit to take
care of the application. The problem with this sort of reasoning
is that it is simply not biblical.

Any study of the preaching of the Old Testament prophets
will confirm that they constantly applied the word that God had
given them for His people. They did so with boldness, often using
what some preachers refer to as "the prophetic *you.*" They did not
say, "*We* need to repent." Rather, they said to their listeners, "*You*
need to repent!" Jesus and the apostles also engaged in pointed
application. They also used the prophetic "you." For years I have
done the same, and I know that God uses this direct approach
to touch the hearts of people.

Whereas explanation deals with the "then" of the biblical text, application addresses the "now" of the text. It uses
present-tense verbs. Again, if I were applying John 3:7, I would

say, "Just like Nicodemus, *you* need to be born again." The "you" is there, and the verbs are present tense and easy to understand.

Conclusion and invitation. After the body of the sermon is completed, the message must be concluded, and the listeners must be challenged to respond to what they have heard through the invitation. If we compare the sermon to an airplane flight, the introduction would represent the takeoff, the body of the sermon would be the actual flight, and the conclusion and invitation would represent the landing. Unfortunately, some pastors conclude their sermons so poorly that their message ends up crashing instead of landing. A great sermon can be nullified if the preacher does not know how to end well.

The conclusion to an evangelistic sermon can be approached in a variety of ways. For instance, the preacher can review briefly the primary points of the sermon body. The conclusion is also an excellent time to share an appropriate, gripping illustration. Also, the sermon's primary theme can be restated, and a primary portion of Scripture from which the message was derived can be quoted again.

The most important part of the conclusion is at the end when the gospel of Christ should be shared and an invitation to receive Christ should be given by the preacher. The primary recipients of evangelistic preaching are non-Christians. God will sovereignly summon sinners to listen if the preacher will preach evangelistically. Lloyd Perry notes that there are usually four types of people in every congregation. These include "believers, . . . apathetic people, people with doubts, and usually some people who are hostile to the gospel."[6] Some of those people are in need of the saving gospel.

The preacher must plan and prepare his invitations in detail. Unless he does, there will not be a smooth transition from the conclusion to the invitation, and the end of the sermon will not be effective. During the invitation of the sermon, the preacher should share about man's sin, Christ's death for man's sin, and man's need to repent from his sin and put his faith in Christ alone as Savior. It is also helpful for the preacher to lead those who want to be saved in a prayer to receive Christ.

Preachers who do not give their listeners the opportunity to be saved at the time the evangelistic sermon is preached are guilty of a great sin against both God and man. People should be allowed to decide about Christ at the moment the gospel is presented. To delay is dangerous. That may be the last opportunity a person has to be saved. If they are not told how to be saved, are not encouraged to be saved, and are not given the opportunity to be saved, when they walk away from that sermon, their blood is on the hands of an irresponsible preacher (see Ezek. 3:17–19).

The preacher should take every precaution to avoid planned, manipulative tactics throughout his sermon, and especially during the invitation. Many of us have cringed as we have witnessed preachers using their "tricks" to get people to come forward during an invitation. If the Holy Spirit is dealing with a person, he simply needs to be guided, not beguiled. So-called "decisions" that come from exploiting people's emotions do more harm than good. Such "commitments" rarely last because they were prompted by "cleverness of speech" (1 Cor. 1:17) rather than the conviction of God's Spirit. A preacher simply needs to share the truth of the gospel, and then lovingly and articulately invite people to receive Christ as Savior.

Public invitations are vitally important. In our day, every ungodly person of every sort is proudly and publicly "coming out of the closet." It is time for Christ's followers to "come out of the closet" as well. Jesus died publicly for us. Is it too much for the preacher to ask converts to acknowledge Christ before others? Absolutely not! For an in-depth study of the public invitation, the reader is encouraged to read the works of Roy Fish,[7] O. S. Hawkins,[8] R. Alan Streett,[9] and Farris Whitesell.[10]

Summary

The late W. A. Criswell, longtime pastor of the First Baptist Church of Dallas, Texas, gives an excellent summary of the necessary characteristics of an effective evangelistic sermon. It must be: (1) biblical in content, (2) simple in construction, (3) personal in concern, (4) winsome in appeal, (5) uncompromising against sin, (6) presented to show pardon in Christ alone, (7) preached with energy and zeal, (8) delivered in marvelous expectancy, and (9) proclaimed with utter reliance on the Holy Spirit.[11] For almost fifty years, that giant of the faith exercised with great effectiveness and skill the art and work of preaching evangelistically in a Baptist pulpit. The result? Thousands were saved for the glory of God!

Indeed, at the heart of any great church is an evangelistic pulpit. If the leader is not evangelistic, preaching persuasively for a verdict, church members will not be inclined to reach people for Christ either. For a church to be on fire, the pulpit must be on fire. A pastor is not to be a thermometer that just registers the spiritual climate of his congregation. Rather, he is to be a thermostat that proactively and aggressively sets the spiritual climate of his flock. While not all Christians are called by God to be vocational evangelistic preachers, evangelism is the responsibility of every Christian. "All are to go, and to go to all."[12]

Preachers plant and water the gospel seed, but they must remember that it is the Lord who "causes the growth" (1 Cor. 3:7) and saves lost people. But preach we must! God will not cause seeds that have never been sown to grow. The gospel seed will not leave the barn by itself, nor will it sow itself. The sower (preacher) must go out and sow the seed, which is the word of the gospel (Mark 4:3, 14). Once it is sown, the sower must water that seed with love, tears, and fervent prayer (Ps. 126:6). It is then that God causes the seed to grow.

This world does not need more feel-good, relational "communicators" who desire merely to dialogue with the culture and their congregations about vague, relative spiritual issues. Instead, we need some modern prophets of God to rise up and proclaim God's Word evangelistically. "Sermonettes breed Christianettes."[13] The purpose of evangelistic preaching is to win people to Christ as Savior and Lord. When a preacher preaches evangelistically, he is not primarily addressing the social or material needs of mankind, nor does he seek principally to instruct believers in righteousness. Instead, his chief goal is to proclaim Christ in such a way that non-Christians are brought under conviction and desire to be converted into faithful followers of Jesus Christ.[14] An evangelistic preacher seeks to lead the lost to Christ.[15]

Preaching evangelistically is both a privilege and a responsibility. Stephen Olford emphatically affirms this by stating, "God has chosen people like you and me to be preachers of the gospel. The awesomeness of this calling is almost overwhelming when we realize that God had only one Son, and He made Him a preacher."[16] The British Methodist preacher, W. E. Sangster, concurs by adding:

> Called to preach! . . . Commissioned of God to teach
> the Word! A herald of the great King! A witness of the
> eternal gospel! Could any work be more high and holy?
> To this supreme task God sent His only begotten Son.
> In all the frustration and confusion of the times, is it
> possible to imagine a work comparable in importance
> with that of proclaiming the will of God to wayward
> men?[17]

The need of the hour in our churches and our nation is for genuine evangelistic preaching. As Paul said, "How then will they call on Him in whom they have not believed? How will they believe in Him whom they have not heard? And how will they hear without a preacher?" (Rom. 10:14 NNAS). Prayer must permeate both the development and the delivery of the evangelistic sermon. The preacher must pray and worship God fervently so that his heart will be ablaze and then study the biblical text in such a way that his head is full of biblical truth. He must also live a life of moral integrity so that the message will be believable.

If a preacher should be able to do anything, he ought to be able to preach. If he preaches, he ought to preach evangelistically. What eternal difference does it make if one's preaching inspires, informs, and entertains but no one is saved? Heaven is calling. Hell is threatening. Lost listeners are waiting. Preacher, why do you hesitate? "Preach the word . . . [and] do the work of an evangelist!" (2 Tim. 4:2, 5).

Chapter 4

Preaching Evangelistically with Biblical Authority

Al Fasol

When God called Moses to return to Egypt as His spokesman, Moses asked an excellent question: Moses said to God, "Suppose I go to the Israelites and say to them, 'The God of your fathers has sent me to you,' and they ask me, 'What is his name?' Then what shall I tell them?" (Exod. 3:13 NIV). Essentially, Moses wanted to establish his authority for speaking not only to the Israelites, but to the king of Egypt as well.

God's response to Moses is the all-time unequaled and unparalleled expression of authority. God said to Moses, "I am who I am. This is what you are to say to the Israelites: 'I AM has sent me to you'" (Exod. 3:14 NIV).

What a wonderful and wonder-some thing to say! "I am who I am!" No one else ever has or ever will be qualified to say such a thing. God is the only one who can say, "I always have been, I am now, and I always will be." The authority residing in those five words—I am who I am—cannot be challenged! The Egyptians had gods. Their gods were nouns, sculpted by humans. Those idols sat on shelves and could do nothing. The sun god could not hear the plaintive pleas of the Egyptians for its blessing. The moon god could not feel the poignant prayers of the Egyptians. The river god could not see the Egyptians kneeling before it. Any other gods they had could not smell the Egyptians' daily offerings of incense and sacrifice to them. Why not? They were only nouns, created by humans.

When God answered Moses by saying, "I am who I am," God identified Himself as alive and active. The Egyptian gods were nouns, but the living God of the universe is a *verb* who responds to and guides His creation. No one or nothing else in the universe can match the authority of those five words from God: "I am who I am." God's answer to Moses is this: I am all the authority you will ever need.

This authority is not to be taken lightly. A little over forty years later, God would also say: "I will raise up for them a prophet like you [Moses] from among their brothers; I will put my words in his mouth, and he will tell them everything I command him. If anyone does not listen to my words that the prophet speaks in my name, I myself will call him to account. *But a prophet who presumes to speak in my name anything I have not commanded him to say, or a prophet who speaks in the name of other gods, must be put to death*" (Deut. 18:18–20 NIV).

Authority is an important issue in preaching. Any preacher may be asked, "By what authority do you say what you say?" Any genuine preacher will be happy to answer that question. Our authority to speak comes from God's call on our lives, and our authority for saying what we say is based on God's holy Word, the Bible. Two kinds of authority questions are at work here: the authority of God and the way our listeners perceive this authority in us.

The Authority of God

The divine call to preach must be exactly that—a divine call. As God said, "I will raise up for them a prophet" (Deut. 18:18 NIV). God clearly warns listeners to hear what the prophet has to say, since the words the prophet or preacher speaks are words that God has commanded be spoken. To speak presumptuously for God is to invite one's own capital punishment.

This divine call to preach must be carried out in the way God said it should be carried out: "I will put my words in his mouth, and he will tell them everything I command him" (Deut. 18:18 NIV).

The words God has given us for these days reside in His holy Word, the Bible. The issue of biblical authority in preaching is always a serious issue. Never is this issue more significant than it is when we are preaching evangelistically.

To preach with biblical authority, and especially to preach evangelistically with biblical authority, means we must be the strongest students possible of God's holy Word. Every preacher must read the Scriptures daily, and every preacher must read all of the Scriptures. That is, every preacher must read the Bible from Genesis chapter 1, verse 1, all the way through to Revelation chapter 22, verse 21. What a sham it would be for a preacher to have read only a portion of the Word and yet expect to speak for God with authority! The Bible's message is full of life. How can a preacher preach from the bread of life when the preacher has tasted only a portion of it and never dined on the full sumptuous spiritual meal that God has placed before us?

The Biblical Text

As the best possible students of the Word of God, we prayerfully select a text from which we feel God would have us preach. What, specifically, is a text? The definition of a text must necessarily be a functional one. A text is *a complete unit of biblical thought*. The text, therefore, may be one verse or sentence as, for example, found in the book of Proverbs. The text may be a paragraph, or a chapter, or more than one chapter. Whatever its length, the text should not be fragmented because that leads to the danger of misinterpreting the text.

The text, whatever its length, is never to be considered apart from its immediate context or its entire context. The immediate context consists of the verses and chapter immediately before it and immediately after it. The immediate context may include the entire book in which it is found. Knowing something of the background of an individual book of the Bible will give light about the meaning of a text found within that book.

The entire context is the Bible itself. The purpose of the Bible is to reveal God. The superior revelation of God is through His Son Jesus. God has chosen to record His revelation in human words which comprise the holy Bible. The purpose of the Bible is to reveal God through His Son so we might know that God's Son is the way, the truth, and the life and that no one will come unto the Father except by Him. No Scripture passage in the Bible stands alone. All of Scripture is intrinsically connected. The primary meaning of any biblical text is found within itself, but the eternal application of any biblical text is found in the entire context of the Bible.

Selecting a text for an evangelistic sermon must be done with care and with prayer. We must be careful to rightly divide the word of truth. The eternal fate of souls is at stake.

Some biblical texts are obviously written as a plea and as instruction for nonbelievers to accept Jesus as Lord and Savior. John 3:1–17 is probably the most popular example of such a text. Luke 15, especially verses 11–24, is another often-used evangelistic text. John 14 is another. Many, but not all, preachers interpret Matthew 1:18–25 and Luke 2:1–20 as evangelistic texts. Other popular passages of Scripture seem to be written to believers but contain instruction and urging for nonbelievers. Ephesians 2:1–10 is an example.

Scripture passages such as Isaiah 7:14 and Isaiah 9:1–7 could possibly be used as evangelistic texts, especially when combined with New Testament passages that fulfill the prophecies of the Old Testament.

The evangelistic preacher must not impose an evangelistic purpose on any text in an awkward way. For example, the Beatitudes in Matthew 5:2–10 are addressed to believers. Many preachers, however, contrive to make a text say something it does not say. Such preachers will say something like: "Blessed are the meek for they shall inherit the earth. But you say, 'Preacher, I am not meek. How do I get meek?' You can't be meek until you accept Jesus as your Lord and Savior."

Or a preacher might look to Matthew 5:13 and say, "You are the salt of the earth! But you cannot be salt until you accept Jesus as Lord and Savior!" These preachers try to build a bridge from the eternal truth of the text to another eternal truth not found in the text. This approximates saying to God, "Good thing I came along when I did, God. You didn't get Your holy Bible written just right, but I will correct that problem for You."

When preaching evangelistically, we must rightly divide the word of truth and declare the eternal truth of Scripture as it is presented to us. When we proclaim the Word accurately, we find the Word is, indeed, a two-edged sword. We need not add to or amend the Bible. We need to proclaim it as it is and let the Holy Spirit make any other applications He wishes to make.

Measuring the Biblical Authority

The relationship between a biblical text and the sermon preached from that text can be evaluated. H. C. Brown Jr. provided seminal work in this area. Brown suggested four categories of biblical authority within a sermon: direct, indirect, casual, and combination. *Indirect* seems an inappropriate word in the context. *Indirect* sounds as if it is the opposite of *direct*. I suggest the categories should be: direct, secondary, casual, and combination.

Direct biblical authority means the relationship between the text and the sermon is strong and clear. To accomplish this, the evangelistic preacher should read the text several times; study what commentators and others have said about the text; and then the preacher should write a simple declarative, past-tense sentence of fifteen to eighteen words interpreting what the text meant when it was written. The next thing the evangelistic preacher *must* do is write a similar sentence but this time in present tense making an application of the text for today. The preacher has now conscientiously moved from the *then* of when the Scripture was written to the *now* of when it is to be proclaimed. In essence, the direct biblical sermons mean that *what the text teaches, the sermon preaches.*

Secondary biblical authority develops *implications* from the text. As an example, Exodus 20:13 has been translated, "Thou shalt not kill." For many interpreters, the word *kill* is better translated *murder.* Some preachers complete the implication of the text by including abortion as murder. The Bible does not specifically mention the destruction of fetal life, but many preachers are comfortable in completing the implication of the verse by including a biblical prohibition of abortion founded on this verse.

Preparation for the secondary biblical sermon closely follows the preparation for the direct biblical sermon: read the text, study what commentators have written, write a statement of *direct* interpretation of the text, and then write a statement interpreting the implication or secondary idea of the text. Both sentences are important. The first sentence allows you to see the direct meaning of the text. The second sentence will be much more intelligently and accurately written when it is monitored by the direct biblical authority sentence.

Casual biblical authority develops some "weaker" or marginal *suggestions* from the text. Philippians 4:22 provides an excellent example: "All the Christians send you greetings, especially those attached to Caesar's household." The direct teaching would be something like, "Christians told each other hello." There is not much we could do with this idea in a sermon. But the apostle Paul has left us with a tantalizing bit of information: *especially those attached to Caesar's household.* The most difficult place in the world to be a Christian at that time had to be in Caesar's household! Yet there were Christians there! Not only that, those Christians sent greetings to other Christians! The suggested sermon here is this: Being a Christian in a difficult place or under difficult circumstances.

Prepare the casual biblical authority sermon in the same way as you would a secondary sermon. The difference is that the second sentence this time is built on a marginal suggestion in the text rather than on a stronger implication of the text.

Combination biblical authority means that part of the sermon may be direct and another part may be secondary or casual. The important thing is that the preacher must be aware when these transitions are made and make those transitions smoothly and without deviating from the text.

The biblical text should always dictate the development of the sermon. This is particularly accentuated when we are preaching evangelistically.

Perceived Authority

The biblical authority residing in our evangelistic sermons should be all the authority we need. The Bible was literally "God-breathed" into existence. God Himself is the great "I AM." The preacher is called of God to proclaim His message. What more authority could be required?

By its very nature, the evangelistic message is addressed to nonbelievers, or to people who have never heard, not accepted, or outright rejected God and the Bible as authority in their lives. These people need to be led to accept God's authority. They need to be led to this point by other believers or, perhaps, by a preacher. To get to this point, the nonbeliever must assign to God's messenger some semblance of authority, otherwise why would they listen to us at all? What kind of authority are they seeking in us, if not the authority of God and His Bible?

The nonbeliever will want to know if God's messenger is a person of *integrity*. The nonbeliever desperately wants to be able to *believe* in the messenger. If the nonbeliever cannot believe in the messenger, then the nonbeliever has no reason to believe the message.

How does the integrity of the speaker become established in the minds and hearts of the non-Christian? No doubt, by seeing the messenger of God living an exemplary Christian life. When the non-Christian sees God's messenger living without rancor and hatred, living within the moral standards established by God Himself, living in respect of the differing religious views within Christianity, living a life of sacrifice to self and in service to others, living a life of love for God, family, church, and others, and living a life prayerfully under the control of the Master, then any person who has not professed belief in Jesus as Lord and Savior will be impressed and will perceive God's messenger as having some authority to speak.

Integrity is absolutely essential. Without integrity no one will perceive God's messenger as having authority to speak about eternal salvation.

The nonbeliever will want to know if God's messenger is a person of biblical and theological *knowledge*. This matter of expertise in our field is also important. Who would ascribe authority to anyone who is not knowledgeable?

When we consult a physician, we want to consult a physician who is knowledgeable rather than one who is weak in that field. When we contract with a builder, we want to make that contract with a person who has knowledge of the building trades. When we hire a lawyer, we prefer to hire a lawyer who knows the intricacies of the law and is capable of achieving a just settlement. When a non-Christian agrees to listen to a preacher, he wants to listen to someone who has committed to studying the

Bible and can communicate what God requires of us accurately and truthfully.

Finally, the nonbeliever will perceive spiritual authority in God's messenger when the messenger communicates a strong sense of *conviction* about the good news of the gospel. The lost person is more likely to ascribe authority to a person who exudes enthusiasm and dynamism about the message being proclaimed. This enthusiasm and dynamism might be proclaimed in what has been called the "shout, stomp, and sweat" style of delivery. This enthusiasm and dynamism may be conveyed in a more subdued manner, but even then the message is communicated with a clear sense of vitality. No one will ascribe authority to a messenger who appears to be complacent. Everyone will ascribe authority to a messenger who has a sense of urgency and immediacy.

Preaching evangelistically means we are proclaiming a message and that the eternal souls of people are at stake. In God's holy name, let us proclaim that message in His authority alone!

Chapter 5

Giving an Evangelistic Invitation

Roy Fish

A theological student from England was sent by a professor to hear a noted preacher on the weekend. He came back with a kind of sophisticated disgust and said to his professor, "That man didn't do anything but say, 'Come to Jesus.'" "And did they come?" his professor gently inquired. "Well, yes they did," the student grudgingly replied. The professor then said, "I want you to go back and listen to that man preach again and again until you can say, 'Come to Jesus' as he did and people respond."

Biblical Basis

"Come to Jesus." This simple invitation contains God's greatest invitation word in the entire Bible—*come*. To an unreasonable and unerring people, God said, "*Come* now, and let us reason together . . . though your sins be as scarlet, they shall be as white as snow; though they be red like crimson, they shall be as wool" (Isa. 1:18 KJV). "*Come* house of Jacob and let us walk in the light of the Lord," He appealed in the very next chapter (Isa. 2:5). God extends a universal invitation in Isaiah 55:1, 3: "Ho, every one who thirsts, *come; come* to the waters; and you who have no money, *come* and buy and eat, yes *come* buy wine and milk . . . incline your ear and *come* unto me." Through the prophet Hosea, God said, "*Come* and let us return to the Lord for he is torn but he will heal us" (Hos. 6:1).

Jesus said, "*Come* after me and I will make you fishers of men" (Matt. 4:19). He appealed universally in the invitation, "*Come* unto me all you who labor and are heavy laden and I will give you rest" (Matt. 11:28). Jesus made clear that coming was the condition for receiving the life He came to offer to us. "All that the father gives me shall come to me and him that comes to me I will in no wise cast out" (John 6:37). The Bible virtually ends with an invitation to *come:* "The Spirit and the bride say *come,* and let him who hears say *come,* and let him who is thirsty *come*; let him who desires take the water of life freely" (Rev. 22:17). God's great yearning and appeal for people to rightly respond to him as a rule is couched in his beautiful invitation word, "*come.*"

Preaching evangelistically is woefully incomplete without an invitation to come to Jesus. In the New Testament it is obvious that evangelistic preaching and compelling invitations were virtually inseparable. The nature of the message preached compelled the herald of the message to appeal for response. It is true there are no instances of invitation without proclamation in apostolic preaching, but it is also true there are also no instances of proclamation without invitation.

The message of Jesus is of such a nature that an invitation to respond is the logical outcome of its declaration. Though the word *come* might not be the precise word of the invitation, the invitation for response was always a part of apostolic preaching. After a sermon at Pentecost, Peter clothed the word *come* in terms of "repent and be baptized" (Acts 2:38). He did essentially the same thing in his second sermon: "Repent therefore and be converted that your sins may be blotted out" (Acts 3:19 NKJV). A loving God makes sinful humanity a concrete offer of forgiveness on the basis of the saving acts of His Son. Such an offer demands a call for decision. The good news of Jesus demands a verdict.

The Essential of Heart Preparation

To some degree, what is said about heart preparation in giving an invitation could be said about evangelistic preaching as well. The preacher who extends an evangelistic invitation without giving serious consideration to the issues at stake makes a major tactical error. C. E. Matthews asks, "How many people realize these facts? It might be said that the majority in the congregation and many of our ministers have little or no concept of the seriousness of the inexpressible importance of the invitation."[1]

It is an awesome thing to confront an individual or a congregation with the offer of the gospel. In challenging preachers along this line, C. E. Autrey says:

> Let him pray until his greatest desire is to see the lost saved. Paul said, "Knowing therefore the terror of the Lord, we persuade men" (2 Cor. 5:11). Lost men are under the wrath of God (John 3:36). They are not aware of their condition. The evangelist knows this and must, by his firm, tender pleas, lead the sinner to realize his guilt before God. Mere perfunctory concern in the evangelist cannot be used of God to bring a sense of dire need in the sinner's heart.[2]

Preparing the heart becomes especially important when one looks through the lenses of eschatology at the immensity of the issues of an invitation. What a sobering thought that everyone to whom we present the good news of Jesus is a person with an eternal destiny! One's response to the gospel invitation determines where he or she will spend eternity. Our finite minds can hardly grasp the implications of this infinite reality. For many people the ultimate choice which will mean eternal heaven or hell for them is made during an evangelistic invitation. As Autrey suggests, these immense issues should be pondered prayerfully by a preacher before he ever goes into his pulpit.

Though the eternal implications of response to invitations far outweigh any other aspect in importance, there is much more involved in one's decision than this. The benefits of the gospel are experienced not merely in the "by and by" but in the "here and now" as well. Jesus came that we might have life abundant in this present world. For instance, many unsaved people to whom the offer of Christ is made are leading very lonely lives. No one can assuage that loneliness like Jesus. Many who sit in church services on Sunday have brought the fragments of broken lives in hope of finding an answer. Jesus can put the pieces of broken lives together again; joy and peace, new and meaningful purpose for life can be experienced by those who make an affirmative response to an invitation to come to Jesus.

The preacher should realize that one's initial step in knowing life of this quality can be made during an invitation. The preacher's mind should be saturated with these facts as an invitation is given.

Regardless of the nature of a sermon, an evangelistic invitation is always appropriate. A brief explanation of the gospel should be shared at the end of every message. Spurgeon is reported to have said, "Before you conclude any message, make a beeline for the cross." There will be other propositions in an invitation, but in preaching evangelistically, no other issue can be permitted to eclipse the appeal to make an immediate response to the offer of salvation.

However, it is not essential to give an invitation the very same way every Sunday. The great C. E. Matthews laments our perfunctory persistence in doing the same thing every Sunday at the end of every service:

> The preacher, as usual, in a cool and collected manner
> announces the number of the closing hymn with the
> stock statement: "We shall sing the first and last stanzas

of the hymn. Should there be those present who wish to unite with the church in the manner in which we receive members, you may come forward as we sing." Could there be a greater tragedy than such a closing of a religious service? It is not inferred that there is any intended wrong in such an invitation, but one is almost persuaded that the devil himself could say amen to such an effort.[3]

Planning an Invitation

Invitations, like sermons, should be planned. I have been acquainted with an evangelist who claims he gives as much time to planning his invitation as he does his message. Having seen him offer a number of invitations, I am led to believe he is not exaggerating his point.

One of the strongest invitations I ever saw was one into which a great deal of planning had gone. The preacher of the evening concluded his message with an illustration about Robert Ingersoll, the noted infidel from Illinois. He related how Ingersoll would speak in cities all across the Midwest. He would speak on subjects such as "Why I Am Sure There Is Not a God," "The Mistakes of Moses," "Why Only a Fool Would Believe in Hell." In turn he would build up straw men and proceed to tear them down.

One night in a midwestern city after Ingersoll had supposedly exploded any possibility that there might be validity in the

Christian faith, he offered a challenge to his audience. He spoke something like this: "I am aware that many Christians come to hear me speak. I would like to ask who in this audience tonight after I have spoken would still claim to be a Christian. After hearing what I have said tonight, is there anybody here who will testify, 'I still believe'?" Not a person stirred. Ingersoll put his hands on his hips and laughed uproariously. He offered the challenge the second time. "Isn't there even one Christian here who will stand tonight and say, 'I still believe after hearing the great Ingersoll'?" Nobody responded. Again, Ingersoll laughed. He offered the challenge the third time.

This time from one of the back rows of the theater two teenage girls stood and began to move slowly down the aisle singing, "Stand up, Stand up for Jesus, ye soldiers of the cross. Lift high his royal banner; it must not suffer loss." As they walked, others slipped out from their seats and followed them until ultimately almost the entire audience was standing as one great throng in front of the stage singing in Ingersoll's face, "Stand Up, Stand Up for Jesus."

As the evangelist told the story, about halfway through, the instrumentalist began to play the song, "Stand Up, Stand Up for Jesus," a somewhat militant invitation hymn. By the time he had concluded the illustration, he went immediately into his invitation and invited all who were willing to stand up for Jesus by receiving him as their Savior and Lord by uniting with his church or by completely yielding to Christ as Master to come forward. I was not surprised when around seventy-five people responded. This represented a superb job of planning an invitation. Don't be afraid of innovation and creativity at this point.

In preaching evangelistically, as in the sermon above, a message should build toward the important moments when people will be invited to decide for Christ. Even at the outset of an evangelistic message, it is wise for a preacher to explain that he will be giving an invitation at the close of his message. To make reference to this in the body of the message is helpful as well.

Planning will result in variety in an evangelistic invitation, something most preachers have never seriously considered. In smaller churches where the pastor preaches to virtually the same congregation every Sunday, a planned variety can do away with a kind of unnecessary monotony in the invitation. In larger churches where there is the possibility of an unexpectedly large numerical response, it is possible that an invitation could be extended for a rather lengthy period. If so, the worship leader should be ready to change the invitation hymn during the invitation. This should be planned ahead of time.

Types of Invitations

As a rule, a preacher should have in mind the manner in which he intends to conduct the invitation. If an invitation is extended for a longer period of time than what is customary, the preacher should have a Plan B to which he reverts. Actually, a preacher could have two or three types of invitations in mind and trust the Holy Spirit to guide him about what order should be appropriate.

There are several possibilities as far as types of invitation are concerned. The New Testament does not prescribe a certain way a person is to indicate outwardly that he is coming to Jesus. The fact that there was a method of public indication that one was deciding for Christ is very obvious, but the prescribed manner is not always the same.

The exact method used in extending invitations in the New Testament was undoubtedly varied. More than once, Jesus simply said, "Follow Me," and this was the extent of His invitation. On other occasions, Jesus said, "Come unto Me." Exactly how Simon Peter called for open declaration of faith at Pentecost is not clearly stated, but the fact that three thousand people were baptized is clear indication that Peter gave people a chance to openly indicate their response; otherwise he would not have known whom to baptize out of the huge crowd that heard him that day.

Invitation to Come Forward

In many evangelistic churches, the standard invitation is an invitation to come forward and be met by someone at the front of the auditorium. Most Southern Baptist churches use this kind of invitation.

There are some caution signals to which churches should give attention when using this kind of invitation. First, it is a dangerous assumption to think that all who come forward have clearly understood the conditions for becoming a Christian and have already met those conditions. It is the opinion of this author that most of those who come in response to an evangelistic invitation are coming as inquirers. They have not yet made a commitment to Jesus and have not yet met Him in saving faith. They should be counseled as "seekers." Only after they have trusted Jesus for themselves should they be presented as potential members coming into the church on confession of faith.

Card Signing

In a day of innovative worship styles, many churches have stopped inviting people to come forward and confess faith. Some of the fastest-growing as well as some of the largest churches in the United States have opted for giving people an opportunity to express interest by filling out a card or signing a perforated section of the bulletin. Such options as "I would like to know more about becoming a Christian," or "Today I prayed to receive Christ as my Savior" can be seen on cards in the backs of chairs or pews along with similar statements on an order of worship.

Many churches that give invitations of this nature wait until the end of the invitation to receive the offering, giving those who signed an opportunity to indicate it by leaving the symbol of their decision, the card, in the offering plate. Churches which use this kind of invitation, as a rule, are very thorough in following up with phone calls or visits to those who have left a signed card in the offering plate.

Some people object to this type of invitation, saying it offers no opportunity for public confession of faith. The argument would likely be followed up with the words of Jesus: "Whoever acknowledges me before men, I will also acknowledge him before my Father in heaven. But whoever disowns me before men, I will disown him before my Father in heaven" (Matt. 10:32–33 NIV). But even a cursory reading of the New Testament, the book of Acts in particular, shows that the essential public confession of faith in the New Testament was baptism. This is the manner of public confession in churches that use cards or similar opportunities of expressing interest.[4]

Counseling or Inquiry Rooms

I was walking out of a large church recently when I saw a large sign that read "Inquiry Room" on a door adjacent to the auditorium. Having grown up in an era of haphazard, hit-or-miss, slipshod counseling of people who came forward in an invitation, I was glad to see the sign and realized it reflects the fact that churches, in general, are taking more seriously the matter of dealing with inquirers.

There are several ways an inquiry or counseling room could be used. First, the pastor could call attention to the room at the end of his message and invite people who are interested in knowing more about the Christian faith to stop by the room after the services are dismissed. Congenial, well-trained counselors would be in the room to greet them. A second way the room could be used would be that of taking people who come forward to the inquiry or counseling room immediately. The pastor, after greeting someone who has come forward, would present him to an appropriate counselor who would take him to the room and talk with him in depth about the decision he is making.

The use of inquiry or counseling rooms necessitates a church having trained counselors who relieve the pastor of the responsibility of dealing with every person who comes forward. If several people respond in an invitation, traffic jams can occur in the altar area, and this can be a hindrance to others coming forward. Overall, an inquiry or counseling room probably provides the most intensive kind of counseling of any method of invitation. Life's biggest decision deserves this kind of thoroughness.

Lifting One's Hand

In days gone by, a popular kind of invitation was one in which people were invited to raise their hands. Using this kind of invitation with tact and discretion, can be of much spiritual benefit to some people who want spiritual help. While the congregation is bowed in prayer, invite all who sense their need and want to invite Christ into their lives simply to raise their hands as an indication that they are making the decision to do so.

Praying Where You Are

Many people who have heard an evangelistic sermon or even an evangelistic appeal would like the opportunity to pray. But many times they don't know exactly how to pray. The pastor should invite all who want to become Christians to follow him as he leads them in a "sinner's prayer." Having explained to them that he is going to lead them in a prayer of acceptance of Christ, he would slowly lead them to pray softly or silently after him a prayer of this nature:

Dear Lord Jesus, I thank You that You love me and that You died to take away my sins. I admit that I am a sinner and I need You as my Savior. Come into my heart right now and forgive my sins. I trust in You to be my Savior, and I depend on You to take me to heaven when I die. I will follow You as my Lord as long as I live. Thank You for hearing my prayer. Amen.

A wise pastor will, as a rule, use more than one of these methods in an invitation. One pastor of a church in the South made use of four of them every Sunday. First, he would invite people who were not Christians or were not absolutely sure to follow him in a "sinner's prayer" as he led them clause by clause from the pulpit. He then would invite all who prayed with him to come openly and confess that they had prayed to receive Christ. After this part of the invitation had ended, he would call attention to the part of the bulletin on which people in the invitation could check a small box or a line indicating they had prayed the prayer with him but perhaps did not want to come forward. His fourth appeal was an invitation to stop by the counseling or inquiry room where they could learn more about what it means to know Jesus personally.

Pastors who serve churches with two hundred or more in attendance should follow this example.

Characteristics of a Good Invitation

Invitations should be extended with confidence. Every message preached and every invitation extended should be done so in the confidence that God wants things to happen and the preacher should expect them. There is a story about a young student who came to Spurgeon and complained that he was not seeing conversions in his preaching. Spurgeon's response was, "You don't expect conversions every time you preach, do you?" The young man replied, "Well, I suppose not." Spurgeon declared, "That's precisely why you are not having them."

Real expectation and confidence in God will seldom be disappointed. Even the very words used in the invitation should express confidence and expectancy. For that reason, it is not honoring to the Lord to say Sunday after Sunday, "Isn't there one person here today who will respond to the claims of Christ and come?" That question should be asked like this: Not "Isn't there one?" but "How many of you here today will receive Christ as your Savior?" Rather than "Won't you come?" make it, "As you come, I will be here to greet you."

In thinking of words used in an invitation, clarity about what the preacher desires should always characterize his appeal. People should be told clearly how to receive Christ as their Savior and Lord. Then with the same clarity, they should be encouraged to make an open commitment that they are receiving Him.

Words something like this should be expressed: "This morning, if you are willing to turn from your sins and trust Jesus

Christ as your Savior, I invite you to slip out from where you're standing and come forward. I will be here at the front of the auditorium to meet you as you come." If one has ever watched evangelist Billy Graham give an invitation, he leaves little question as to what he wants people to do and precisely how he wants them to express the fact that they are doing it. The preacher should leave no question in the minds of hearers about how he wants them to respond.

Urgency should characterize any invitation on the part of the preacher who is preaching evangelistically. The New Testament says, "Behold, now is the accepted time; behold, now is the day of salvation" (2 Cor. 6:2 KJV). Until a person responds affirmatively to Jesus as Savior and Lord, he is living in rebellion against Him. Jesus is a king who is the rightful ruler of every person's life. Until people positively decide for Him as Lord and Savior, they are living in revolt against the king. People should not be encouraged to leave the service without being brought face-to-face with their responsibility of responding to Christ. We should not invite them to go away and think over whether they are to receive Him or not.

A classic story out of the life of Dwight L. Moody has to do with an experience in which he gave his hearers the opportunity of leaving the service to meditate on the question, "What will you do with Jesus?" At the close of the sermon, he said, "I wish you would take this text home with you and turn it over in your minds during the week and at next Sabbath we will come to Calvary and the cross, and we will decide what to do with Jesus of Nazareth." Then he turned to Ira Sankey and asked him to sing a closing hymn. Sankey sang:

Today the Savior calls,

For refuge now draw nigh;

The storm of justice falls

And death is nigh.

The next morning much of Chicago lay in ashes because it was on that Sunday night of October 8, 1871, that Mrs. O'Leary's cow kicked a lantern over and the great Chicago fire began. Many of Moody's congregation died in the fire. To his dying day, Moody regretted that he had told the congregation to wait. He later testified:

> I have never dared to give an audience a week to think
> of their salvation since. If they were lost, they might
> rise up in judgment against me. I have never seen that
> congregation since. I will never meet those people until
> I meet them in another world. But I want to tell of one
> lesson I learned that night which I have never forgot-
> ten; and that is, when I preach, to press Christ upon the
> people then and there, and try to bring them to a deci-
> sion on the spot. I would rather have that right hand cut
> off than to give an audience a week now to decide what
> to do with Jesus.[5]

Every preacher should learn a lesson from Moody's painful statement. Give an invitation with urgency.

Chapter 6

Hiding Behind the Cross As You Preach

Al Fasol

O̲ur mission as evangelistic preachers is to know the truth and to communicate the truth. These are lifetime disciplines. In this chapter we will talk about knowing the truth a little and about communicating the truth a lot.

Preaching is a theologically integrative discipline. An effective preacher is a lifetime student of the Bible, of biblical languages, and of the historical and geographical background of the Bible. An effective preacher is a lifetime student of biblical, systematic, and historical theology and the attendant disciplines of history, philosophy, and Christian ethics. An effective preacher is an effective interpreter of the Scriptures, rightly dividing the word of truth.

Preaching is also a communicatively integrative discipline. The effective preacher is a lifetime student of rhetorical principles, developing sermons clearly and with contemporary appeal. The effective preacher is a lifetime student of people, studying how and why people receive oral communication, knowing that some prefer to hear explanation of a biblical passage, while others love to hear applications of a biblical passage, and both love to hear illustrations to better understand and feel the explanation and application of a biblical passage.

The effective preacher is a lifetime student of speech, including vocal production or clarity of enunciation, pronunciation, and articulation; the use of rate, pitch, volume, and pause to communicate what the hearers are to feel as well as what they are to know; body language, which supports and enhances the oral presentation; and oral interpretation, which is especially helpful in making the reading of the biblical text of the sermon a major highlight in the worship experience. The effective preacher is a lifetime student of communication principles which, among many other things, tell us predictability in either content or delivery what drastically reduces the impact of a message.

The need for effectiveness in these various disciplines is accentuated when we are preaching evangelistically.

The purpose of the Bible is to bring people into eternal life through faith by grace which we receive from our Lord and Savior, Jesus Christ. That purpose transfers to and informs our own ministries as Christians. This purpose is largely achieved through oral communication. The goal of this chapter is to guide us to a level of communication in which the listeners mentally "see" what we are saying. In doing so, the listeners lose "sight" of us, but that is fine because then they are "seeing" Jesus. This accomplishes what the apostle Paul had in mind in 2 Corinthians 4:5: "For we preach not ourselves, but Christ Jesus the Lord; and ourselves your servants for Jesus' sake" (KJV).

On every Lord's day, tens of thousands of preachers pray, "Lord, hide me behind the cross as I preach." This chapter will provide instruction on how any Christian communicator can accomplish exactly that. Our premise is this: The purpose of sermon delivery is to maximize the message and minimize the messenger.[1] This, again, is accentuated when we are preaching evangelistically.

Full Vocal Production

Foundational to all good oral communication is full vocal production.[2] The process of vocalizing is a complicated one. Speaking is overlaid on breathing which means many things are happening at the same time when we speak. We are forced to discuss these many things one at a time, but remember that when we speak, they are happening all at the same time.

Full vocal production is frequently referred to as "diaphragmatic speaking." This is misleading. How many times have you been told or heard someone being told, "Speak from down here!" pointing to where their diaphragms would be. This is misleading and confusing because our larynx or vocal cords are located in our throats and not in our abdomens. Full vocal production refers to the various parts of our anatomy used in speaking that work together to produce the clearest vocal sounds we can make.

The diaphragm is a thin band of muscle located just under our lungs. As we inhale, if we are inhaling properly, the expansion of our lungs pushes the diaphragm down. This causes a chain reaction. The diaphragm pushes against the stomach and rib muscles. These muscles respond by pushing the diaphragm back to its original position which in turn squeezes the lungs that are full of oxygen. This squeezing process increases the air pressure in our lungs, allowing us to exhale comfortably. With a slight tension on our vocal cords, we make sounds as the oxygen passes through. We may continue vocalizing this way until our lungs need more oxygen, and so we pause, take a breath, and continue speaking.

When we speak, we vibrate the air outside of our mouths. These vibrations are vocalized sounds that we hope can be interpreted intelligently. We need to remember, though, that just as the air outside of our mouths is being vibrated, so the air remaining in our lungs is also being vibrated. That vibration, or reverberation, in our lungs gives our voices resonance or "depth."

Each of our vocal cords has its own unique structure. Thick vocal cords vibrate more slowly, causing a lower or bass vocal tone. Thin vocal cords vibrate more rapidly, causing a higher pitch or tone. In addition to our vocal cords, the vibrations in our lungs, our throats, our nasal cavities—even the shapes of our skulls—all contribute to what is eventually heard as our individual speaking voices.

The vocal cords are delicate. Persistent dryness of the vocal cords and persistent strain on the vocal cords cause problems such as a gravelly rather than a clear voice. Eventually, abuse of the vocal cords could cause problems severe enough that we may have to not speak for an extended time. Dryness is caused by too much air being expelled as we speak. We must use our stomach muscles to control how much pressure is put on the diaphragm and lungs and, therefore, how much air is used as we exhale and speak.

Strain on the vocal cords is caused by speakers tightening their throat muscles in order to project their voices. When the voice is used in this way, some attention is drawn to the speaker rather than to the message. It is much better to speak with a strong, clear voice and let the listeners concentrate on the message rather than the messenger.

God has equipped us to be able to speak loudly, with urgency, with conviction, and with unction several times a day without straining our vocal cords. You can preach, say, four or five times on Sunday and still not have a "sore throat." Your brain will be tired, your legs will be tired, and your back will be tired. But your voice will still be clear, and you will not feel a soreness or strain in your vocal cords when you start using full vocal production.

So many preachers have gravelly voices that many people mistakenly feel that is the way a preacher is supposed to sound. Many of the gravelly voiced preachers will smile and say, "I guess I preached my heart out each time I preached." The heart is not what they preached out. It is their voices they "preached out." But God has equipped us so it is not necessary to preach our voices "out."

Vocal Variables

The heart of the heart of a style of sermon delivery that will hide us behind the cross as we preach lies in the uses of the vocal variables. The four vocal variables are pitch, volume, rate, and pause. When used to support the content of our messages, the vocal variables will cause our listeners to "see" what we are saying. As we have already noted, "seeing" what we are saying means they do not see us. We are hidden behind the cross as we share a message from the Bible. The first three of the vocal variables work together at the same time to convey our messages. Pauses allow the vocal variables to be understood and then interpreted. Since our listeners are forced to use mostly hearing to receive our messages, we must do everything we can to help them receive our messages in the ways we intend for them to be received.

Pitch

Pitch covers a lot of territory. Pitch may refer to our individual voice quality or to a certain key in singing. We are primarily interested in this chapter in how pitch can support the content of our messages. Therefore, we will think of pitch in terms of vocal *inflections*. Vocal inflections guide people to understand which words in our messages are more significant than other words. Vocal inflections also alert people about whether we are making a statement or asking a question. Vocal inflections guide our listeners about whether they should have negative or positive feelings about what they are hearing.

For instance, inflections with a slightly higher pitch can be used at the beginning of a sentence to convey that a new sentence or a shift in thought is occurring. An inflection with a slightly different higher pitch will be used at the ends of some sentences to convey that the sentence is a question rather than a statement. Inflections with a slightly higher pitch can be used throughout the sentence to indicate something light, pleasant, or even amusing is being said.

Inflections with a slightly lower pitch will communicate a sense of seriousness, or even something foreboding. An inflection with a slightly lower pitch is used at the ends of sentences to indicate that it is the end of a sentence.

Various levels of inflections will be used by various speakers at different times for various reasons. Listen to a tape of yourself communicating an evangelistic message and see if your words sound as if they support your message in a clear manner. Try repeating some of the sentences, but place the inflections on different words to see if that more accurately communicates the message you were trying to convey.

Volume

Volume essentially means speaking loud enough to be heard. Volume should be adapted to the size and acoustics of any room in which we speak. Volume also must be used in support of the words in our messages. Some words call for higher or stronger volume, and other words do not.

Higher volume is most often used to emphasize a word or phrase. With higher volume the listeners can understand and appreciate the emphasis being placed on that thought and thereby assign that thought the importance it deserves. Some speakers will use a lower volume to make an emphasis. When using lower volume, our delivery will need extra help from body language. This will be discussed later.

The important thing to remember is that volume is not an end in itself. Many of our listeners have heard preachers whose philosophy was, "No matter what I say, I yell!" Two things are wrong with that statement. First, to speak at the same volume level is only to achieve a mono-volume. That approach does not support content. Second, speaking at the same volume level consistently calls more attention to the speaker than it does to the message. By yelling all the time, you succeed only in magnifying the messenger and minimizing the message.

Use variety in volume. The variety will be dictated by the content of the message, and in that way you will maximize the message by alerting the listeners about how they should feel about the message they are receiving.

Rate

Rate refers to how rapidly or how slowly we speak. Experts who make a study of such things inform us that the average rate of speech in the United States is 125 words per minute. That seems mighty fast to some people and somewhat slow to others.

How fast or how slow we speak, however, is not as important as relating our rate of speech to the content of our messages.

Generally, a little more rapid rate is used when we are sharing something that is familiar, or is easy to understand. Slower rate is used when we are sharing something not so familiar, is a little more complicated, or when we are making an emphasis. Each of us will have to determine an average rate of speech that is best for our listeners and is best for us individually.

Pauses

Pauses involve a sense of "timing." This sense operates differently in each of us. These individual differences are related to our individual differences in the use of rate. Brief pauses, certainly less than a second and up to one second in length, are commonly used to separate sentences. Longer pauses are used on occasion to give time for an important idea to be fully absorbed. On some occasions, long pauses of three to five seconds are used just before stating an important idea. (Warning: when using a dramatic lengthy pause, do not announce beforehand, "I am going to drop a bomb on you." That warning will defuse the "bomb." Let the content have its own explosive results. Also, when using a dramatically long pause, be certain you have something important to say!)

Many public speakers have developed a sense of timing in which their most effective pauses come at a time when they need to consult their notes. All speakers should learn to do this.

No one can dictate to individual speakers how long or short the pauses should be. We must develop our own sense of timing.

Give yourself a little test with the vocal variables. See if you can say the same words in two different ways. See if you can say the same words and convey two entirely different messages. For example, pretend you are to give a ride to someone you love dearly. Think, perhaps, that you are to pick up a child after school. The parking area around the school is crowded. Dozens of children are streaming out the main doors. You see your child in the distance and wave. As your child approaches, you happily say, "Hello, there. Get in. Let's go!" To communicate your joy and eagerness, you will use inflections with a little higher pitch. Your volume will be just loud enough to be heard over the general commotion. You do not speak rapidly or slowly, and the pauses are short.

Let's change the circumstances. Suppose your child caused some problems at school that day. The school counselor called you and requested that you do something about it. You see your child coming out the door. You wave. As your child comes close to the car, you say the same words but with an entirely different meaning. You still say, "Hello, there. Get in. Let's go." This time you say the words with hardly any inflection. Your volume is at a lower, more deliberate level. Your rate is definitely slower, and the pauses are longer. This time instead of communicating happiness and eagerness, you are communicating disappointment and sending warning signals. The content is exactly the same. The difference is that the vocal variables changed the meaning.

That is how and why vocal variables are the heart of the heart of communicating in such a way that our listeners can receive our messages clearly. Good use of the vocal variables is the most important way to hide ourselves behind the cross whenever we speak, but especially when we are preaching evangelistically.

Body Language

Body language is almost as important as vocal variables if we are to communicate our evangelistic messages effectively. Body language, for our purpose, consists of eye contact, facial expressions, gestures, and posture. Body language is communicated by sight and therein lies an important fact. Excuse a rough analogy, but body language travels at the speed of light—around 186,000 miles per *second*. The content of our messages travels at the speed of sound—around 720 miles per *hour*. The first impressions our listeners receive is from body language.

Body language, like the vocal variables, must support the content of our messages and must be used in strong conjunction with the vocal variables. Body language tells the listeners what they should feel about the message they are hearing. In many ways body languages assist in telling them what they should know from the message they are hearing.

Eye Contact

Eye contact with our listeners is important. Listeners like to know the speaker is aware of their presence, and they like to think by their own body language that they are helping the speaker deliver the message. By looking in the general direction of a group of people, you will make each of them feel that you are making direct eye contact with them, even though you have actually made direct eye contact with only a few of them. Every listener wants to feel that eye contact has been made several times.

Strive to be looking at the listeners around 90 percent of the time. Seventy-five percent would be a minimum acceptable level. During the 10 to 25 percent of the time you are not looking at listeners, take that opportunity to look at your notes. Be careful not to drop eye contact as you are finishing a sentence. Wait until you have completed the sentence, and then drop your eyes to look at your notes.

Do not look over the heads of people. Some speakers have been told to look over the heads of people if looking at people makes them nervous. Looking over the heads of people is distracting and makes it less likely the listeners will make a positive response to the message.

Moving around the pulpit area, or the platform, or wherever you may be speaking is fine, but as you move be sure to maintain good eye contact.

Facial Expressions

Facial expressions help listeners understand how they are to feel about a message. Often when children are asked about a preacher, they respond by saying something like, "He had a happy message, but he looked like he was mad the whole time." Facial expressions should at least suggest how the listeners should receive the message. A smile does not have to be a broad grin to convey to listeners that this part of the message is pleasant, and it should be received positively. A frown does not have to be a scowl in order to communicate a sense of disapproval. A blank expression will cause the listeners to think we do not care how the message is received. As always, let your content dictate what kind of facial expressions, and how many, need to be used.

Gestures

Gestures involve the use of our arms *and* hands. Gestures especially add to the listeners' comprehension of what they should feel as well as what they should know. If the speaker says something like "Jesus died for people throughout the world," he can make a rounded gesture as if he were tracing the outline of a globe.

The best gestures are full arm gestures. Avoid keeping the elbows too close to the sides of the body. Picture a football referee signaling an incomplete pass. Notice how the referee uses a sweeping motion with both hands. Picture how ineffective the signal would be if the referee kept his arms pinned to his side and used only a half gesture.

Gestures help the listeners "see" what is being said to them. The use of gestures that do not relate to the message, or the use of ineffective half-arm gestures, cause people to notice the messenger rather than the message.

Posture

Posture is important because it conveys our inner feelings. If our inner feelings are that we are delighted to share an important message from God, our posture and what is sometimes described as our "general demeanor" will communicate that feeling. This is shown not only in how straight we stand but also by a slight leaning toward the listeners. This slight leaning toward the listeners sends a signal of a sense of urgency in what we are about to say and a sense of eagerness and comfort in being the person who is proclaiming that message.

By placing one foot slightly in front of the other and putting our weight on the forward foot, we achieve that slight leaning toward the listeners. The added benefit of this posture is that it prevents the speaker from shifting weight from one foot to another, resulting in a swaying motion that is always distracting.

The purpose of body language is to assist the listeners in understanding and in feeling the message they receive from anyone who is preaching evangelistically. Body language should support the message in such a way that we are hidden behind the cross as we speak.

Oral Interpretation

Oral interpretation is both a science and an art. It is a science because we can suggest a way for everyone to experiment with reading the verse to accomplish effective oral interpretation. It is an art because even when we conduct this experiment, we use some subjectivity in how we do so.

Oral interpretation seeks to communicate the meaning as well as the feeling of a biblical text. A simple exercise will help accomplish this. Take any full sentence from any book of the Bible. Say the sentence aloud several times, and each time emphasize only one of the words. Let's take John 3:7 as an example: Jesus said, "Do not marvel that I said to you, 'You must be born again'" (NKJV). Say the verse aloud and put great emphasis on *Jesus*, and then use a monotone on each of the other words. Next, say the sentence again, this time placing great emphasis only on the word *said*. (Note the comma after *said*. A punctuation mark is a good sign that a short pause is needed.) Say the sentence a third time, and put emphasis on the word *marvel*.

As you recite the verse this way several times, you begin to appreciate how the vocal variables can help you convey the meaning of the verse to the listeners. What you are doing is using the vocal variables so that listeners can come alive to the Bible. Your oral interpretation will guide them to feel what the passage has to say to them. When they do so, the reading of Scripture becomes a highlight in the worship experience.

Chapter 7

Examples of Evangelistic Sermons

Communications experts and educational programmers inform us that people learn in four different ways: auditory, visual, kinesthetic, and tactile. For each of us, one of these ways of learning is prominent. The auditory learner likes to be mentally challenged and to receive information. The auditory person likes explanation of the text. The visual learner likes analogies and anecdotes. This enables the visual to "see" what the preacher says. The visual learner likes explanation by illustration and application by illustration. The kinesthetic person likes to participate. This is the person who will encourage from the pew with a vociferous "Amen!" The kinesthetic wants to know how to put the explanation of the text into action. The kinesthetic learner likes application of the text. Tactile learning plays a small role, if any, in preaching.

The auditory, visual, and kinesthetic learners are reminiscent of the famous saying of the philosopher René Descartes. Descartes's oft-quoted phrase is: "Cogito ergo sum" or "I think, therefore I am." That describes the auditory. The visual could be described as "Video ergo sum" or "I view" or "I see, therefore I am." The kinesthetic could be described as "Sentio ergo sum" or "I feel, therefore I am."

Each of these different types of learners is present in all congregations. The majority of our listeners these days are probably kinesthetic. Contemporary congregations want to "feel" or "experience" the truth. However, these feelings need to be based on information, so no sermon, including the evangelistic sermon, should be without the foundational explanation of the text. The visuals need illustrative material to help them "see" the truth, but auditory and kinesthetic listeners also benefit by illustrative material.

The sample sermon below incorporates these three kinds of appeals.

"What Do You Mean by Sin, and What Do You Mean by the Cross?" by Al Fasol
Romans 6:23

The man standing at the doorway of my office didn't bother to say "Hello" or "How are you?" Instead, he said, "Before you say anything, I want to know, what do you mean by sin, and what do you mean by the cross?"

The "man" is one of my best friends. Let's call him Tom. Tom stood there in his air force uniform, a full bird colonel, and he was standing militarily erect with a somber expression on his face. Tom is about six feet two inches tall and ordinarily wears a brilliant smile. On this day, Tom was dead serious.

What did I do? I jumped from my chair and hugged him and said, "Tom, you scamp, get in here and let's talk." I had been looking forward to this day for seventeen years. Tom and I first met in college. After graduation Tom joined the air force. He spent more than five years as a prisoner of war in Vietnam. Tom was the first person to whom I witnessed when I became a Christian seventeen years before.

At the time, Tom smiled and said he was happy for me, but being a Christian meant nothing to him. Just before he was shot down and captured, though, he wrote me and said, "That which happened to you needs to happen to me. I guess I am more aware of my mortality now than ever before. As soon as I get home, talk to me about being a Christian." And now, finally, we talked.

I opened my Bible to Romans 6:23 and handed the Bible to Tom for him to read. Tom said he had never held an open Bible in his hands until then, and then he read the verse: "For the wages of sin is death; but the gift of God is eternal life through Jesus Christ our Lord" (KJV).

Tom has always been a curious person, hungry to learn and to know. That's why I felt led to dig a little deeper into the Word than I ordinarily would in a witnessing situation. I said,

"Tom, that word *wages* has an interesting history." I saw his eyes brighten a little and was encouraged by that. I continued: "Tom, the original meaning of the word *wages* is something approximating 'cooked meat' or 'cooked provisions.'" Tom wrinkled his nose but leaned forward with eagerness in his eyes and asked, "Cooked meat! How in the world can you get from cooked meat to wages?" I was so glad he asked.

I shared briefly how the word we translate as *wages* appears in some fragments of ancient letters dating all the way back to the time of Alexander the Great. We have to surmise some of the details, but the history was something like this: Alexander ordered his troops to conquer a city, or village, or territory, or whatever, and then he would try to befriend those conquered. A military officer, for instance, might attach himself to the household of the governor of the conquered people and promise to pay restitution for damages incurred in the battle.

However, the letter fragments seem to indicate the officer wrote to the emperor and advised that the people did not need money. The agricultural fields were devastated in the battles, and the food supplies were low. So they suggested that instead of money they be sent food—cooked meat or cooked provisions. The officer then might have said something like, "I promised you money, but you don't need money. Instead of money, let me give you a substitute pay; let me give you cooked meat or cooked provisions." The word was used in that way so often that we could probably translate verse 23 this way: "For the substitute pay of sin is death, but the gift of God is eternal life through Jesus Christ our Lord." That is very likely how the people in

Rome understood the word when this letter was read to them back in the first century.

Tom was totally taken in. He said, "The word *sin* is next, and that is really my question. Does it have a word history too?"

"More of a word picture than a word history," I told him. The picture is one of missing the mark. Sort of like when a pilot aims a missile at a bridge or an ammunition dump, but the missile explodes short of the target.

Tom chimed in right quick that yes, he could understand that analogy. He reflected on how the missile would explode into millions of pieces; in fact some of the pieces were vaporized. Tom said his life is like one of those missiles. He came home to find his wife was not waiting for him. He came home to find he had no home. He came home to find his life had been vaporized.

I told Tom that God would provide him a new life. We looked at John chapter 3 for a while, but then Tom came back to Romans 6:23. He said, with a little edge in his voice, "You and the Bible are wrong." Well, he caught me off guard. I asked what he was talking about. He read the first part of the verse again and said, "I have sinned, and I am not dead. I have seen you sin, and you're not dead. Obviously, you and the Bible are wrong because people sin all the time but they are not dead."

Tom misunderstood what the Bible means. He thought of this death as a physical death rather than a spiritual death. After brief, prayerful thought, I told Tom a bit of family news. I told Tom my mother had died when he was a POW. As college classmates we went to each other's homes occasionally. Tom and my mom got along just great. Tom was saddened to hear of her death. I mentioned to Tom that my sister stood looking at Mom in her casket for a long time. I asked her what was going on. She said, "I am just talking to our mom." The point of all this is that before death we could talk to Mom and she would respond. Now we could talk to her, but we could get no response.

I told Tom this described his situation with God. Because of the substitute pay of sin, Tom could talk to God, but God could not answer. Why? Because the substitute pay of missing the mark is the death of the relationship you had with God. Your sin put it to death, but there is one way that relationship can be restored, and that is through the gift of God spoken of in the second part of the verse.

"Before you go there," Tom said, "you still haven't answered my question about the cross."

I had Tom turn to Romans 5:6–8. Tom was reluctant to read the passage aloud, but I insisted. When he did read it, he spoke the words in a bored monotone. I realized that we had been talking for a long time and he was a little mentally fatigued. Because of that fatigue, he missed the message of those beautiful words: "For when we were yet without strength, in due time Christ died for the ungodly. For scarcely for a righteous man will one die: yet peradventure for a good man some would even dare to die. But God commendeth his love toward us, in that, while were yet sinners, Christ died for us" (KJV).

To get Tom to relax a little, I felt led to ask him some questions for a while. Tom liked that. First question: Were any of the POWs executed while you were there? He did not know for certain. He heard that some were, but he did not know for certain. Second question: If you had the opportunity, would you have died in their place? Tom seemed a little perplexed by the question and said no, he did not even know those guys. It is not like they were close friends or anything. Third question: Suppose I were a POW with you, and I was to be executed. You and I are acquainted. You and I are best of friends. Would you have died in my place? I could tell the question angered him, and his answer was no he probably would not have died in my place, and I probably would not have died in his place either. Fourth question: Suppose a Vietnamese antiaircraft gunner was to be executed for whatever reason. Would you have died in his place? With a sneer Tom said that was a stupid question. Nobody dies for his enemies.

I smiled and Tom knew he had missed something. I told him I thought he was now ready to read those verses again. He did. When he finished, I started expanding on their meaning, telling him we were Christ's enemies when we sinned or rebelled against Him. Then I realized Tom was not hearing a word I said. I watched him for a while. His eyes were glazed with a happy, delighted look. Finally, he came out of this little trance and said, "I never knew there could be a love that deep!" I knew this was the moment I had been praying for those past seventeen years.

Suddenly Tom came out of the trance and said a little belligerently, "I still have another question!" I nodded to him, and he softened a little as he said, "I don't really know how to ask this. I guess I can't figure out why you all choose Jesus to worship. I can't figure out why you chose Him and not some of the other people who were crucified. I can't figure out, in any case, what the death of a man two thousand years ago has to do with me today." He kind of shrugged his shoulders as if to say, Can you help me?

I assured Tom he had asked an excellent question and told him I would answer in two ways. First, when Jesus died on the cross, it wasn't the form of execution that was important. I know we see lots of crucifixes, but it wasn't the form of His execution that was important. What was important is that Jesus arose from the dead. That blew Tom's mind, and we talked about that for a while before coming back to his question.

I told him that when Jesus died, it was as if He said to Satan, "Satan, you are allowed to gather all the power you can gather from every sin that has ever been committed, is being committed today, and all the power you can gather from every sin that ever will be committed. You are allowed to exercise that tremendous amount of power on Me today." Satan did, and the impact of all that sin, including yours and mine, killed Jesus. But three days later He arose from the dead and said, "All the power of sin and all the power of death are not enough to conquer Me!" That is why we worship Him. We did not choose Him; He revealed Himself to be the Son of God.

Second, you were not far away when you heard me pray to receive Jesus as my Lord and as my Savior. While I was praying, it was as if I were in chains and each link of the chains that enslaved me was forged by each of my sins. I tried so hard to be a better man on my own, but I never could make it. I tried so hard to build peace in my life on my own, and I never could make it. I tried so hard to break those chains, but I never could do so. That's why I turned to Jesus. With Satan pulling on those chains as hard as he could, I prayed, "Dear Jesus, I am so sorry for what I am and who I am. I have sinned against You repeatedly and at time without shame. But God, I am ashamed now, and I need You. Please, God. If what I have heard and read about You is true, please save me. Please, accept me as Your child and let me live my life for You from this day on."

We couldn't see it, but when I prayed, Jesus was in the room, and He said to Satan, "I have heard this prayer, and I have purchased this soul with My own blood. Satan, let him go!" And Satan had no choice but to let me go.

"Why?" Tom asked. "Why did he have to let you go? What if Satan had said, 'I won't let him go'? What then?" I could tell Tom was a little worried for himself. I told Tom, "Remember, Satan hurled all the power at his command at Jesus, but that was not enough to conquer Him. Satan has no bargaining power. His power is all used up, and it wasn't enough to defeat Jesus. Satan is depleted before Jesus. Satan has no choice but to do what Jesus tells him to do. And that goes for you right now, Tom."

Tom shook his head. Tom said, "Maybe another day, but not today."

This is not how this sermon is supposed to end. For a long time, though, that was the end of this sermon. Thirteen years later, Tom and I were together, and he asked to go through this conversation again. We did. After that he took about fifteen minutes by himself. When he returned, he shared with me that he had just asked Jesus to save him, and He did. After thirty years, two months and nineteen days of prayer, Tom came to know Jesus as Lord and Savior.

That is Tom's story. What is important now is your story. You have heard the struggle and questions of one man. His questions are questions all of us ask and for which all of us need answers. The answers you heard were God's answers, taken from His holy Word. Tom's story has not ended yet. Tom is on a journey that will take him into eternal life though Jesus Christ our Lord. What Tom did is what you need to do.

I want you now to come and accept Jesus as your Lord and Savior. If you still have questions, I want you to come now and ask me those questions. From God's Book we will find the answers you seek.

. . .

The narrative above is a detailed synopsis of how this sermon was actually preached. Let's notice some things about this sermon.

The biblical authority is *direct*. The expository method used to explain the text clearly relates to what the two biblical passages say. As far as the explanation of the text is concerned in this sermon, what the text teaches is what the sermon preaches.

Notice how the introduction first speaks to the auditory listener by introducing the title in the first paragraph. Everyone knows, especially the auditory learner, that this sermon will be about sin and about the cross. The next paragraph describes Tom in some detail. The visual learner especially appreciates being able to see these distinguishing characteristics about Tom. The visual person will dearly love this type of sermon because the sermon is actually an extended illustration that conveys information about the text.

The kinesthetic learner does not find direct application of the text until the conclusion/invitation. Ordinarily, this would be disturbing to the kinesthetic learner, but since the sermon is centered on a human interest situation, and since all of the explanation of the text is in the context of a man's struggles and questions, the kinesthetic listener finds it easy to "participate" in the sermon.

Notice also how the introduction makes a connection with the listeners. The most vital issues in life—sin and the cross and what they mean to us—are discussed from the opening sentence. The title also conveys the subject or concern of the sermon. The text was not introduced until the beginning of the body of the sermon, but the other two purposes of an introduction— connecting with the listeners and introducing the subject of the sermon—were accomplished.

Notice the body of the sermon is built on movement rather than points. If the sermon had been preached in two points, the thought pattern would have run the risk of being separated or divided. With the narrative style of the sermon, the same exegetical information that is often brought out in a rhetorical, point-by-point style is brought out without breaking the flow or movement of the sermon.

The invitation is specific and pointed directly to the non-believer. The synopsis of the invitation perhaps is a little misleading in that these thoughts surely were more thoroughly developed than indicated here. The synopsis does tell us the preacher was headed in the right direction for developing a strong, clear invitation.

God the Evangelist
Loving People the Way God Loves Us
Risky Business by Ralph Douglas West
Romans 5:6–8

Cathy Ames is described in John Steinbeck's *East of Eden* as a monster, misshapen and horrible. Beautiful physically, distorted psychologically. According to Steinbeck, a girl like Cathy would have been considered possessed by the devil. She lives up to his literary description. She is a murderer, betrayer of love, and a worthless mother. But her vices become her virtues. After she is beaten and left for dead, the thin golden-haired girl crawls up the steps of Charles and Adam Trask's farmhouse. Adam cleans the dried blood from her lacerated lips and swollen face. Adam's heart is taken by the helpless blue-eyed monster. He woos her, marries her, and carts her off to the Salinas Valley.

She gives birth to twins and abandons her home without naming, nursing, or nurturing her sons. Fifteen years elapse, and Caleb has heard that Kate, the madam at Faye's whorehouse, is really his mother. Dogging her steps for several days and noticing the resemblance of his mother in the face of his brother, he brokers a conversation of inquiry with Chinaman Lee, the family butler.

One night Lee, tapping away at his typewriter, heard a quiet knock on his door and let Cal in. The boy sat down on the edge on the bed, and Lee let this thin body down in the Morris chair.

Cal spoke softly and rapidly. "I know where my mother is and what she's doing. I saw her."

Lee's mind said a convulsive prayer for guidance. "What do you want to know?" he asked softly.

"I haven't thought yet. I'm trying to think. Would you tell me the truth?"

"Of course."

The questions whirling in Cal's head were so bewildering he had trouble picking one out. "Does my father know?"

"Yes."

"Why did he say she was dead?"

"To save you from pain."

Cal considered. "What did my father do to make her leave?"

"He loved her with his whole mind and body. He gave her everything he could imagine."

Does that scene awaken another story that we find ourselves in, the story of rejection and redemption? The story of the Bible is the story of a loving God and fallen man. Whatever else we may say about the Bible, it is God's love letter to a world that He desires to save. Karl Barth was once asked, "What is the greatest thought you ever had?" Barth answered: "Jesus loves me, this I know, for the Bible tells me so."

Love is vulnerable to a fault. And the love of God for His creation is without exception. Conversely when Paul penned this word in his love letter to you and me, he was calling us to attention. Attention, this is how much God loves you. These words say, remember the geometry of love God has for His people. Remember the height of God's love, the width of God's love, and the depth of God's love for you and me.

Jason Tuskes was a seventeen-year-old high school honor student. He was close to his mother, his wheelchair-bound father, and his younger brother. Jason was an expert swimmer who loved to scuba dive.

He left home on a Tuesday morning to explore a spring and underwater cave near his home in west central Florida. His plan was to be home in time to celebrate his mother's birthday by going out to dinner with his family that night.

Jason got lost in the cave. Then, in his panic, he apparently got wedged into a narrow passageway. When he realized he was trapped, he shed his metal air tank and unsheathed his diver's knife. With the tank as a tablet and the knife as a pen, he wrote one last message to his family: "I love you Mom, Dad, and Christian." Then he ran out of air and drowned.

A dying message—something communicated in the last few seconds of life—is something we can't ignore. God's final words to us are etched on a Roman cross. They are blood. Red. They scream to be heard. They, too, say, "I love you."

The risk in God's message to the world is that Christ died for us with no guarantee that we would reciprocate the grace gesture.

The death of Christ is risky business. Consider what Paul tells us about the death of Jesus. He reminds us that Christ died for the utterly undeserving. This verse reveals the unflattering terms in which we are described. We are depicted as "helpless" (v. 6), unable to deliver ourselves; second, we are called "ungodly" (v. 6) because of our revolt against the authority of God; third, we are called "sinners" (v. 8) because we have missed the mark of getting right with God, however carefully we may have aimed at it; and fourth, we are called "enemies" (v. 10) because of the hostility between us and God. What a devastating description of man in sin! We are failures, we are rebels, we are enemies, and we are helpless to save ourselves.

There is a poem titled, "A Mother's Heart" that tells the story of a young man who gave his love to a vicious woman. She demanded of him as proof of his love that he bring to her his mother's heart to feed her dog. The young man took a knife, killed his mother, and cut out her heart. As he was running back to the evil woman, the young man fell, and his mother's heart flew from his grasping hand. As her heart rolled past, he heard his mother's heart cry in a still small voice, "Are you hurt, my child, are you hurt at all?"

If a mother's love can be depicted poetically, the love of God can be heard prophetically, "Father, forgive them, for they know not what they are doing." Greater love has no man than this, than to lay down his life for his friends.

Yet the truth is that it is for such people that Jesus Christ died.

> Alas! and did my Savior bleed,
> And did my Sovereign die?
> Would He devote that sacred head
> For such a worm as I?

Was it for crimes that I have done
He groaned upon the tree?
Amazing pity, grace unknown,
And love beyond degree!

Well might the sun in darkness hide,
And shut his glories in,
When Christ, the mighty Maker died
For man the creature's sin.

Thus might I hide my blushing face
While His dear cross appears;
Dissolve, my heart, in thankfulness!
And melt, mine eyes, to tears!

Isaac Watts

We ourselves would hardly die for a righteous man—somebody upright in his conduct—though perhaps for a good man—warm and attractive in his goodness—some people would dare to die.

In Ernest Gordon's *Miracle on the River Kwai,* the Scottish soldiers, forced by their Japanese captors to labor on a jungle railroad, had degenerated to barbarous behavior, but one afternoon something happened.

A shovel was missing. The officer in charge became enraged. He demanded that the missing shovel be produced—or else. When nobody in the squadron budged, the officer prepared to follow through on his threat. Then, finally, one man stepped forward. The officer put away his gun, picked up a shovel, and beat the man to death. When it was over, the survivors picked up the bloody corpse and carried it with them to the second tool check. This time, no shovel was missing. There had been a miscount at the first checkpoint.

The word spread like wildfire through the camp. An innocent man had been willing to die to save the others! The incident had a profound effect. The men began to treat each other like brothers.

When the victorious Allies swept in, the survivors, human skeletons, lined up in front of their captors. But instead of attacking their captors, they insisted: "No more hatred. No more killing."

Sacrificial love has transforming power.

Although this was a courageous act, rarely will a person die for a good man. But God in His divine conjunction demonstrated His love toward us while we were still sinners.

But God shows His unique love for us, in that while we were still sinners Christ died for us. Not for the coldly upright, nor even for the warmly attractive and good, but for sinners—unattractive, unworthy, undeserving. And remember that God does this with no guarantee that we will love Him in return. Here are several proofs of God's love that are worth remembering.

Christ Died to Forgive Our Sin

Twenty-first-century human beings are no longer troubled about their sins. They regard this category as a hangover from the primitive past. They think they have outgrown such a concept.

Words like *sin, guilt,* and *shame* are no longer widely used in many circles, but does that mean the realities to which they referred have disappeared? I think not! In fact, if you listen to today's twenty-first-century human beings describe their situation, you'll notice that words like *phobia, complexities,* and *neurosis* punctuate their conversations. In my opinion, they are referring to the same realities once described by the older names. What has changed is not our human situation but simply our terminology.

We may not like words like *sin, unworthy, enemy,* but we cannot deny that something is going on within us and that the same response has to be made to this turbulence.

Few people saw as deeply into life in the twentieth century as the poet T. S. Eliot. In his lengthy work entitled, "The Cocktail Party," he pictures a woman named Celia talking to her psychiatrist, Reilly, about a certain thing she has done that is really bothering her conscience. Reilly asks her, "What was the point of view of your family about the word *sin?*"

She replies that she had been taught to disbelieve in it, to think of misbehavior as simply "bad form," and to regard anyone who was overly concerned with guilt as a bit "kinky." But then she admits that she had been unable to dispose of her sense of personal failure so easily. She says, "I continue to be bothered by a feeling of uncleanness, a feeling of emptiness, of failure toward someone or something outside myself. And I feel I must . . . atone, is that the word? Tell me, can you treat a patient for such a state of mind?"

Here is the poignant evidence that today's men and women are indeed in trouble about their sins, although they might not use the word anymore. How do we go about dealing with our sins, guilt, and shame?

I have seen people attempt to handle this problem in a variety of ways. The most common, I suppose, is the strategy of evading and avoiding sin, of finding a sense of failure so painful that one represses it and hopes in childlike fantasy that it will go away. The warning in the Bible rings clearly here: "Be sure your sin will find you out" (Num. 32:23).

I have seen other people attempt to get rid of sin by disclaiming responsibility for it—like Adam did when he passed the blame to Eve, and Eve did the same thing by pointing a finger at the snake. This is a way of saying, "It was not my fault. Someone else did this to me and made me do it."

Another strategy for dealing with sin is trying to justify it by saying that many people do the same thing—so why get so upset? This is a very common practice, but it cannot succeed because it comes at the problem of sin from a wrong perspective. After all, the profound realities of right and wrong have never been determined by a popular vote.

The noblest strategy for dealing with sin is the way of self-punishment. Do you remember how T. S. Eliot's Celia said, "I feel I must atone for this"? This is a deep impulse of the human spirit—to conclude that because a wrong has been done, some price needs to be paid or some equivalent action must be taken. Like the blood stains on Lady Macbeth's hand, sin will not be removed by anything we do.

We either accept the atonement God has provided us in Jesus Christ, or we attempt to enact our own atonement. The only way to put away our sin is to bring it to the cross of Christ.

As one self-made man said, "If I had it to do all over again, I'd call in some help." That is the best suggestion I know of in relation to the problem of sin. Call in help—God's help—here and now.

Christ Died to Reveal the Character of God

As human beings we reveal our character by our action, and so does God. God has revealed Himself supremely by giving His Son to die for us. Twice in Paul's love letter to the Romans, he wrote of the demonstration of God's character of justice and love in the cross. In Romans 3:25–26 and Romans 5:8, Paul declares that in and through the death of Jesus Christ, God has given a clear, public demonstration of both His justice and His love.

The ways of God are often viewed by man as unjust. The seeming injustice of God's providence is a dominant theme that runs through the Bible, particularly in the wisdom literature. Why do the wicked flourish and the innocent falter? A Kushneranian philosophy of why bad things happen to good people? There is evidently a need for vindication of the justice of God, a justification to man for the apparently unjust ways of God.

The Bible responds in two ways. It points to the future final judgment, when all wrong things will be righted. And it points us back to the decisive judgment that took place on the cross.

No one can now accuse God of condoning evil and committing injustice.

How can we believe in the love of God in a world filled with so many tragedies? I am thinking of personal tragedy and natural disasters, worldwide poverty and hunger, tyranny, torture, disease, and death. How can the sum of human misery be reconciled with a God of love?

Christianity offers no glib answer to these agonizing questions, but it does offer evidence of God's love, which is just as historical and objective as the evidence that seems to deny it—namely, the cross. The cross does not explain calamity, but it gives us a vantage point from which to view it and bear it.

God demonstrated His love toward us. His love is emphatic, His own love for us. His love is unique; there is no other love like it. God gave His Son for us. Christ died for us. By sending Christ, God was not sending someone else, a creature or a third party. He was sending His own Son; He was sending Himself.

God gave His Son to die for us. It would have been wonderful if God gave us His Son only to become a human being and live among us. But He went further—even to the death of the cross—to the torture of crucifixion and to the horror of bearing sin and feeling forsaken by God.

God gave His Son to die for our sins—for people whom Paul goes on to describe as "sinners," "ungodly," "enemies," and "powerless" (Rom. 5:6–10).

But God in sending His Son gave Himself to die for His enemies. He gave everything for those who deserved nothing from Him. And that is God's own proof of His love for us. So we have been given in the death of Jesus Christ not a solution to the problem of pain but solid evidence of the justice and love of God, in the light of which we may learn to live, love, serve, suffer, and die.

Christ Died to Conquer the Power of Evil

M. Scott Peck said in his book *The Road Less Traveled* that evil is *live* spelled backwards. Peck is saying that there is evil wherever there is life. There is external wickedness as well as internal evil. Where there is life, you are bound to find resident evil. Before evil became a popular psychological theme, it was the theme of life that God sent His Son Jesus to radically deal with.

A cursory reading of the New Testament fills the heart of the reader with the joyful atmosphere of confidence that stands out against the insipid religion that often passes for Christianity today. There was no defeatism about the early Christians; they spoke of victory. For example: "Thanks be to God! He gives us the victory through our Lord Jesus Christ" (1 Cor. 15:57 NIV). "In all these things we are more than conquerors" (Rom. 8:37 NIV).

Victory, conquest, triumph, overcoming — this was the vocabulary of those first followers of Jesus. They attributed this victory to the cross.

We are not, therefore, to regard the cross as defeat and the resurrection as victory. Rather, the cross was the victory won. The resurrection endorsed, proclaimed, and demonstrated that victory.

The cross of Christ is God's only self-justification in such a world as ours.

We can love people if we remember that God loved us with no guarantee that we would love Him in return.

. . .

The biblical authority of the above sermon is *direct*. The exposition of the text is couched in the series of illustrations throughout the sermon. The exposition of the text, wherever it occurs, deals with the text in a direct way.

The sermon opens with a story with which some listeners could identify and all could sympathize. The first sentence sets the tone for the introduction. The rest of the story is told in such a way that the listeners get a mental picture of the characters involved and see the difference between genuine love and genuine hate.

The transition to the body of the sermon begins with another captivating sentence: "Love is vulnerable to a fault."

The body of this sermon also has movement rather than point divisions. The movements are achieved by an intricate balance of explanation by illustration, explanation of the text, and application of the text.

The transition from the body of the sermon to the conclusion is done smoothly: "Christianity offers no glib answer to these agonizing questions, but it does offer evidence of God's love, which is just as historical and objective as the evidence that seems to deny it—namely, the cross."

The love of Jesus for His people is clearly explained, the illustrations have a strong relationship to the "spirit" of the text, and the application confronts the listeners.

Lost! by L. R. Scarborough
Luke 19:10

I want to preach tonight on one word. Considered in the light of eternity, it is the most distressful word in all the languages of men. God uses this word in His Book just a few times. He uses it three times or more in one chapter, and then He uses it to describe the chief object for the life, the humanity, the death, the ministry, the resurrection, and the eternal purpose of Jesus Christ. In the fifteenth chapter of Luke, God describes the search for a lost sheep on the part of the shepherd. He describes the search for a lost coin on the part of a woman. He describes the search of a father for his lost son. When the son was found and came back to his father's house (the Father in that parable represents God in His great fatherly concern for a lost world), he said, "This my son was dead, and is alive again; he was lost, and is found" (Luke 15:24 KJV). There is no way of understanding that Scripture unless you say that God is trying to tell and describe the spiritual condition before God of every unsaved man. He said the boy was "dead." There is no evidence in that parable that the boy had been actually dead and buried. He is talking the condition of his soul. He said he was "lost" and is found. There is no evidence in that parable that the boy was actually lost from human habitation. The fact is he had too much company of the bad sort. He is describing the spiritual condition of his son. In Luke 19:10 He says, "For the Son of man is come to seek and to save that which was lost" (KJV).

The word I want to talk to you about tonight is descriptive of the spiritual condition of every man and woman who has not trusted Jesus Christ as their Savior. It is that little word "*Lost*"—L-O-S-T—Lost. Considered, I say, in the light of eternity and in the light of its spiritual meaning, that is the darkest word in the history of languages. It means separation from God. It means eternal dwelling in the land of eternal punishment. It means the opposite of heaven. It means the extreme opposite of righteousness. It means hell. It means separation from God. It means no peace. It means no happiness, no joy. It means separation from the good and companionship with evil. It means all there is that is wrapped up in darkness, into which no sun shines. It means the starless night of eternity. It means sunless day forever and ever. It means all there is in the punishment of sin, in the wrath of God, in the indignation of a wrathful Sovereign. Lost! Lost! Lost!

Soul-loss the Worst Loss

I saw a man seventy-two years of age standing one morning on the curbstone looking over the smoldering ruins of a block on which stood the day before a magnificent department store but which in the night had gone up in smoke and burned down in flame. As I stood there with my arms about him, he said,

"Preacher, that represents the accumulation of a lifetime. I have lost my *fortune*."

I stood by the bedside of a young man twenty-seven years of age, who six weeks before weighed two hundred pounds. He at that time weighed only about a hundred pounds. He said, "Six weeks ago I had never taken a dose of medicine in my life and so far as I now remember had never had the services of a doctor to ease a pain in my body. But in the last six weeks," he said, with tears running down his manly face, "I have lost my *health*."

I was on the train. A little woman with four children sat across from me. For hours the little baby in her arms, nervous, restless, crying, had wracked her strength; and she sat there unable to care for the child. I tenderly asked her to let me take the child, and for a half hour I walked up and down the aisle of that flying train with the little dirty baby in my arms. My arms were steady, and I was not nervous and disturbed. Finally the tired baby went to sleep in my arms. I laid it down in front of the weeping, tired mother, and she broke down in tears. And I said, "My friend, what is the matter: is there anything else I can do for you?" Amid her sobs she said, "Did you see that man in the front coach chained to the seat?" I said, "Do you mean that crazy man?" She said, "Yes, he is my husband. For ten years we have lived in others' love. We are taking him to the asylum. He has lost his *mind*." She said, "A thousand times I had rather bury him than for him to have to lose his mind."

A few months ago there came to my office in Fort Worth a beautiful woman. I had never seen her before. She knocked on my door and entered and said, "I want to see you privately. I wish you would lock the door." She sat in the chair across the desk from me—a beautiful, charming woman. She said, "I have come across the state to tell you the saddest of stories because I believe in your prayers and your faith in God." That woman sat there and told me a story of her ruin. She said, "Only one other in this world knows the story of ruin I am to tell you now. My fond husband, my precious mother, my own little darling child do not know it." That woman and wife and mother there unfolded to me a story of her own ruin. She said, "I have lost all. Last night in this city I turned to my lips the poison to take my own life." She said, "I am a Christian woman. I have got faith in God, but I have lost my *character*." Said she, "I came out of one of the sweetest homes you ever knew." I looked at that broken heart. I looked on that wrecked home and that wrecked life, and I said, "It is a tragedy to lose one's fortune. It is a tragedy to lose one's health. It is a tragedy to lose one's mind." But I tell you, my friends, it is a tragedy of tragedies to lose one's *character*.

But I am looking tonight into the faces of men and women who are in a worse fix than if they had lost their fortune or their health or their mind or their character. They have lost souls. You have lost souls—a soul that will never die! Death will heal the loss of a fortune. Death will heal the loss of the mind. It will heal the loss of the health. Death will heal the loss of a character. But I will tell you, my friends, there is no healing except in the blood of Jesus Christ for the loss of the soul.

I shall never forget an experience that came to the little town in West Texas where I lived. The little town was made up of cowmen and their families. Late one afternoon the word came in that a little child five years of age had wandered away from a traveler's camp. There were no fences in those days. There was just here and there in all that great expanse a cow ranch. There were scarcely any roads, no farms, no towns—a wide, wild country. I will never forget that night. Every man and every boy spent the whole, live-long night in those woods looking for that child. I will never forget the mother of that child as she wrung her hands when we came about the camp, crying for her lost baby, her little girl that had wandered away. I will never forget the morning that we found the child. I will never forget that night while I live.

My friends, we did not search those woods that night because it was the child of a rich man. This man was as poor and his family was as ragged and neglected as I ever saw. The little girl was in tatters and as dirty as I ever saw a child when we found her. We did not look for that child because she was good. She went away from the camp because she got mad and threw rocks at her mother and went away in a rage. I will tell you why we looked for that child. It was because she was lost. That is exactly why Jesus came from heaven, gave up His throne and power and became man and submitted to the disgrace of taking on human flesh and suffered the persecution and died on the cross and was buried and rose again from the grave. It was to save men not because they were rich or good but because they were *lost!*

The Sinner's Spiritual Condition

Now I wonder with this introduction if you will let me tell you what God says is your spiritual condition before Him.

There are two kinds of sinners in this world, and there is nobody in this world that is not a sinner. Any man who says he is not a sinner runs in the face of the Word of God. There are two kinds of sinners. There is the *saved* sinner and the *unsaved* sinner. That is the way God classifies them. The saved sinner is the man or the woman who has given up his or her sins on a genuine experience of repentance, who has for himself or herself, not through some preacher or priest, trusted the Lord Jesus Christ for himself or herself. In the church or out of the church that man or that woman is saved. That man is a *saved* sinner. And every man or woman in this world who has not had that experience of Jesus Christ formed in his heart by faith is a *lost* sinner, in the church, in the pulpit, or out of it. If the Pope of Rome at his death has never trusted the Lord Jesus Christ as his personal Savior, he will go to hell. If the pastor of this church has not trusted the Lord Jesus Christ as his personal Savior, or does not do it, he will go to hell. And if he does trust the Lord Jesus Christ as his personal Savior, thank God, there are not devils enough out of hell to carry him to hell. My friends, I want to clear your hearts tonight of the rubbish about sin. I have collated here and am going to read you the Scriptures on the unsaved man's spiritual condition before God. This is not some other man's words. It is the Word of God—the word of Jesus Christ. I want tonight to build in this great audience, with the sympathetic prayer and attention of God's people, a genuine scriptural ground for a great revival of religion. If you put it on any other ground, it will blow away with the gentle zephyrs.

Psalm 51:5—"Behold, I was shapen in iniquity; and in sin did my mother conceive me (KJV)."

Psalm 58:3—"The wicked are estranged from the womb: they go astray as soon as they be born, speaking lies" (KJV).

Oh, that doctrine that men are born innocent and can be trained and raised up into Christianity has no sanction in the Word of God.

I have heard the story of a Christian man who said he was going to make a demonstration. He said that a man was born innocent and pure and that he by education and the right sort of home training could be raised up into the kingdom of God. He said, "I will make a demonstration of it." And he got two rattle-snakes—a male and a female. He raised them away from other snakes and fed them on chicken meat and allowed nobody to tease them. From those snakes he raised the eleventh generation of snakes. He said, "The eleventh generation of snakes will have no poison in it, because," he said, "I have educated the poison out of it." They grew to be good sized snakes. One morning he left the cage open. His little boy went out into the yard to play. Playing about the cage he put his hand into it; and those snakes, true to their nature, coiled, rattled, ran out their tongues and struck; and their fangs went into the arteries of that boy, and he died. You can take that snake and put it yonder under the throne of God, by the side of the tree of life, and it will coil and rattle and stick out its tongue and strike at a passing angel.

And I tell you, every man and woman born into this world was born with a sinful nature, and you have got to take that out or they will go to hell. I am going to meet you at the judgment bar of God, and I want you to get used to the truth down here because you have got to meet it up yonder.

Romans 3:23—"For all have sinned, and come short of the glory of God" (KJV).

Ecclesiastes 7:20—"For there is not a just man upon the earth, that doeth good, and sinneth not" (KJV).

Ephesians 2:3—"Among whom also we all had our conversations in times past in the lusts of our flesh, fulfilling the desires of the flesh and of the mind; and were *by nature the children of wrath*, even as others."

God's Word says that the man or the woman born into this fallen race is a child of wrath by his nature.

Ephesians 2:1—"And you hath he quickened, who were dead in trespasses and sins" (KJV).

Ephesians 2:12—"That at that time ye were *without* Christ, being aliens from the commonwealth of Israel, and strangers from the covenants of promise, *having no hope*, and *without* God in the world" (KJV).

Listen to this awful word.

In my pastorate at Abilene years ago in a great revival which I was holding in my church, I went as my custom was to see the people. I went into a hotel which was under a new management. I went into the office and invited the proprietor who had just come to the town to make our church his church home. He was a big, fine-looking man. He looked me in the face and said, "Are you the pastor of that church?" I said, "I am"; and for two or three minutes I stood and heard him swear and curse preachers and churches and Christians. Then he walked back into the private room of his hotel. During that meeting God led him back from twenty-seven years of backsliding, and his wife as well, who was led there by this wicked man. I led to Christ his son, who now, thank God, is preaching the gospel in California. I led to Christ his daughter who is a student in our training school at Fort Worth.

When that meeting was over, one day my telephone rang. That wife at the other end of the line said, "Come." I went to that hotel. I went into that family room. There stood the weeping wife and the sorrowing children. There lay that big strong man on his bed breathing his last. He had been suddenly taken with an incurable disease. His lips moved, and his wife said, "Put your ear to his lips and hear what he says." I am sorry I did. A thousand times his dying words have rung in my soul: "Dying without hope; dying without God; dying without Christ—hopeless, hopeless!" For twenty-five times, I guess, his strength enabled him to say it; and then he went out into eternity.

I want to tell you while you are living, God says you are without Christ and without hope if you have never trusted Jesus Christ as your Savior. John 3:18: "He that believeth on him is not *condemned:* but he that believeth not is *condemned already,* because he hath not believed in the name of the only begotten Son of God" (KJV).

You do not have to be condemned. Your condemnation is in the fact that you have rejected Jesus Christ, and you are condemned now because you have not believed in the name of the only begotten Son of God. You are not going to hell, my friends, because you murdered somebody or because you lied or have stolen or have sworn. You are going to hell for the root of the whole matter, that you have not trusted Jesus Christ as your Savior.

Oh, tonight the memory that comes across thirty-six years! Thirty-six years ago I hung my soul at eleven o'clock one day on John 3:36. Thank God, it has been hanging there ever since. John 3:36: "He that believeth on the Son hath everlasting life: and he that believeth not the Son shall not see life; but the wrath of God abideth on him" (KJV). God help you to see tonight that your soul is lost because you have rejected Jesus Christ.

Jeremiah 17:9—"The heart is deceitful above all things, and desperately wicked: who can know it?" (KJV).

Isaiah 38:17—"Behold, for peace I had great bitterness: but thou hast in love to my soul delivered it from the *pit of corruption*: for thou hast cast all my sins behind thy back" (KJV).

Oh, my friends, I want you to see sin tonight.— *Sin, sin, sin!* I want you to see the sin that was born in your soul, the sin that contaminates your spirit, that makes you swear and lie and have a passion and steal and be dishonest. *Sin, sin, sin, sin*! I want you to see it tonight. It is in your soul. You are a child of the devil by nature. Have you become a child of God by faith? You are lost, lost, without God and without hope!

The Bright Side of the Picture

Now, I want you to look at the other side of that Scripture. "The Son of man is come to seek and to save that which was lost." One side of the picture is sad. It is *Lost, lost, lost!* The other side of the picture is the *cross*, the *cross*, the *cross* of Jesus Christ. Thank God, He says, "*is* come." That means tonight He is here. I saw Him night before last and last night. I saw Him this afternoon. I saw Him thirty-six years ago. I have seen Him in tens of thousands of cases in these last twenty-five years in which I have been trying to preach for Him. I have seen Him come and seek and save and redeem. I bless God tonight that He has power in His blood to take every particle of stain that sin has made in the darkest soul and cleanse it. I bless God for the cleansing power of the blood. This Scripture says that He is seeking.

I want you to think for a moment of the seeking Savior. He is seeking you through your mother. He is seeking that unsaved man tonight by the godly life of his wife. He is seeking that wayward, wicked father by the life of his consecrated daughter or son. He is seeking you through this preacher, through these singers, through this sermon, through His divine Spirit. Why, this tabernacle and these lights are saying, "Come to Jesus." These Christian people say, "Come to Jesus." This civilization in which we live today says, "Jesus is come to seek and to save that which was lost." He is seeking you, and He bids you seek Him. You are a sinner; He is a Savior. You are going to hell if you hold on to your sins. He says, "Hold on to Me. Trust Me. Give me your heart, and I will give you a heaven down here and a great eternal heaven up yonder. Oh, tonight let this Savior come into your soul by giving up your sins and trusting Jesus Christ as your Savior. Tonight, not on the church, not on the ordinances, though I love them; not on a moral life, though I prize it; not on liberality, though I bless God for liberality; but tonight on the two arms of the cross of Jesus Christ I swing out the hope of the world's salvation. "There is no other name in heaven or on earth whereby, you must be saved." Thirty-six years ago I trusted Him; and, thank God, though I have buried my loved ones, I have stood by the bedside of my sick wife and children and other loved ones; I have suffered, but tonight I say, "I do not want any other name." Jesus Christ's name is sufficient.

God help you tonight to let Jesus Christ come to that dark word of your heart where it says "LOST" and let the word *Jesus* be written in its place.[1]

· · ·

The text for this sermon is the final verse of the brief story related to Zacchaeus.

The biblical authority for this sermon is direct. Scarborough does reverse the order of the words of the text. He emphasized the last word of the text, *lost*, not only by placing it first in the sermon but especially by using the word as the title to his sermon. In so doing, Scarborough did not alter the intent of the text and preached the sermon with direct biblical authority.

Scarborough used a limited amount of exposition of the text. This particular verse does not necessitate a great deal of exposition. The historical background of the text is clear, the grammatical structure of the narrative is uncomplicated, and the key words of the text are easily understood. For that reason, this sermon relied heavily on explanation by illustration and by the use of other passages of Scripture as cross references to affirm and reinforce the illustrations.

Scarborough uses strong, clear, direct application. Notice, especially in the concluding paragraphs, his emphasis on the word *you*. (If he had said, *I*, or even *we*, his application would have been inaccurate. If he had said *he, she, or they*, his application would have been ineffective.) This is especially strong in his closing sentence which served as an excellent lead-in to his invitation. Scarborough was especially strong in making the application an emotional as well as in intellectual appeal. This is a good example for all preachers but especially when preaching evangelistically. Much has been said and written about overemphasizing emotions. Scarborough clearly sets forth the biblical information and then builds on that with an emotional appeal. One without the other leads to confusion and uncertainty. Scarborough's use of application helps the nonbeliever both to understand and to feel what needs to be done to become a saved person instead of a lost person. That is application at its best.

The sermon is not built on points, although the published sermon does indicate three divisions in the sermon. These divisions simply guide the listener's thought process about the text. The introduction itself, and the first division "Soul-Loss the Worst Loss," which Scarborough refers to as introductory material, set the stage for the direct application of the text which appears in the next two divisions of the sermon.

The objective of the sermon is clearly evangelistic, and that objective is accomplished with direct biblical authority.

Endnotes

Chapter 1

1. C. H. Spurgeon, *The Soul-Winner: How to Lead Sinners to the Saviour* (Grand Rapids: Wm. B. Eerdmans Publishing Company, 1963), 106–7.

2. Richard Stoll Armstrong, *The Pastor As Evangelist* (Philadelphia: Westminster Press, 1984), 21.

3. Herschel H. Hobbs, *New Testament Evangelism* (Nashville: Convention Press, 1960), 3.

Chapter 2

1. George G. Hunter III, *The Contagious Congregation* (Nashville: Abingdon Press 1979), 22–25.

2. Walter C. Kaiser Jr. and Moiés Silva, *Introduction to Biblical Hermeneutics* (Grand Rapids: Zondervan, 1994), 27–28.

Chapter 3

1. Lloyd M. Perry and John R. Strubhar, *Evangelistic Preaching* (Eugene, Ore.: Wipf & Stock Publishers, 2000). Section 3, "Selecting Material for Evangelistic Preaching" is helpful.

2. Quoted in Lewis Drummond, *Spurgeon: Prince of Preachers* (Grand Rapids: Kregel Publications, 1992), 295.

3. Haddon W. Robinson, *Biblical Preaching: The Development and Delivery of Expository Messages* (Grand Rapids: Baker Book House, 1980), 20.

4. In their compelling book *Famous Conversions*, editors Kerr and Mulder give fifty concise accounts of conversions dating from the apostle Paul to Chuck Colson. Cf. Hugh T. Kerr and John M. Mulder, *Famous Conversions* (Grand Rapids: Eerdmans, 1983).

5. John R. Bisagno, *Letters to Timothy: A Handbook for Pastors* (Nashville: Broadman & Holman Publishers, 2001), 159.

6. Lloyd Perry, "Preaching with Power and with Purpose," *Christianity Today*, February 1979, 23.

7. Fish is a coauthor of this book and has written an excellent chapter herein dealing with the invitation. See also Roy Fish, *Giving a Good Invitation* (Nashville: Broadman Press: 1974).

8. O. S. Hawkins, *Drawing the Net* (Nashville: Broadman Press, 1993).

9. R. Alan Streett, *The Effective Invitation: A Practical Guide for Pastors* (Grand Rapids: Kregel Publications, 1995).

10. Faris D. Whitesell, *65 Ways to Give Evangelistic Invitations* (Grand Rapids: Zondervan Publishing House, 1945).

11. W. A. Criswell, *Criswell's Guidebook for Pastors*, (Nashville: Broadman & Holman, 1980), 236.

12. Arthur T. Pierson, *Evangelistic Work* (London: Passmore & Alabaster, 1892), 12.

13. Quote attributed to both G. Campbell Morgan and Stuart Holden in John R. W. Stott, *Between Two Worlds* (Grand Rapids: Eerdmans, 1982), 294.

14. Roy H. Short, *Evangelistic Preaching* (Nashville: Tidings, 1946), 14–16.

15. Lloyd Perry, *A Manual for Biblical Preaching* (Grand Rapids: Baker Book House, 1965), 2.

16. S. F. Olford, "The Power of Preaching," *Christianity Today* 23 (Dec. 1979): 22.

17. W. E. Sangster, *The Craft of Sermon Construction* (Grand Rapids, Michigan: Baker Book House, 1981), p. 24.

Chapter 5

1. C. E. Matthews, *The Southern Baptist Program of Evangelism* (Nashville: Convention Press, 1956), 93.

2. C. E. Autrey, *Basic Evangelism* (Grand Rapids: Zondervan Publishing House, 1959), 132.

3. Matthews, 93.

4. Just for the record, indicating interest in knowing more by signing a card is not new. The mid-nineteenth century Baptist evangelist Absolom B. Earle used this kind of invitation in his evangelistic crusades.

5. From Clarence E. Macartney, *The Greatest Questions of the Bible and of Life* (Nashville: Abingdon-Cokesbury Press, 1948).

Chapter 6

1. For a comprehensive discussion of sermon delivery, see my book *A Complete Guide to Sermon Delivery* (Nashville: Broadman & Holman Publishers, 1996).

2. See ibid, chapter 1.

Chapter 7

1. This sermon originally appeared in Lee Rutland Scarborough, *Prepare to Meet God: Sermons Making the Way to Christ Plain* (Nashville: Sunday School Board of the Southern Baptist Convention, 1922), 16–29.